Read & Understand

Grade 1

WITH LEVELED TEXTS

Writing: Jill Norris
Content Editing: Joy Evans
De Gibbs
Copy Editing: Carrie Gwynne
Art Direction: Cheryl Puckett
Cover Design: Liliana Potigian
Illustration: Don Robison
Design/Production: Yuki Meyer

EMC 3441
Evan-Moor®
Helping Children Learn

Visit
teaching-standards.com
to view a correlation
of this book.
This is a free service.

Correlated to State and Common Core State Standards

Congratulations on your purchase of some of the finest teaching materials in the world.

For information about other Evan-Moor products, call 1-800-777-4362, fax 1-800-777-4332, or visit our Web site, www.evan-moor.com.

18 Lower Ragsdale Drive, Monterey, CA 93940-5746. Printed in USA.

CPSIA: Printed by McNaughton & Gunn, Saline, MI USA.[7/2016]

Contents

How to Use This Book

1 Make the Story Booklets

Reproduce each story and make booklets for individual students. Use the booklets to

- read to a group.
- have partners or small groups read together.
- have individual students read independently.

The stories support Guided Reading levels C through H, with text ranging from short simple sentences with many repeated words (for emergent readers) to a series of simple and complex sentences (for early readers).

2 Build Background

Relating a story to prior knowledge and experiences helps students better comprehend the story. Ask questions that invite students to tell what they know. For example:

- Before reading *What Will I Take?*, ask students to tell what they would pack to stay overnight someplace and why they think those things are important to take along.
- Before reading *I Have a Ticket*, ask: *Have you ever gone someplace and needed a ticket to get in? What place was it? What kinds of things did you see and do there?*

Concrete experiences also help students develop knowledge of a subject and its related vocabulary. For example:

- Before reading *Shake Pudding*, bring in the ingredients for instant pudding and let the students try making their own "shake" pudding.
- Before reading *The Pet Show*, invite each student to bring in a toy animal to have a pet show in the classroom.

3 Preview the Story

- Read the title of the story and have the students repeat it. Run your finger under the words as you read them to emphasize left-to-right movement.
- Introduce the words in the story's Picture Dictionary and encourage students to watch for the words in the story. Write the words on the board as you talk about them or ask students to locate a word on a specific page.
- Go through the story page by page. Have students look at the illustrations and ask them to predict what they think is happening on each page.

4 Read the Story

When reading the story to students for the first time, read with expression and pronounce words clearly. Invite students to read repeated or familiar words, phrases, or sentences with you. Then encourage students to read lines independently.

5 Do the Skill Pages

Use the skill pages after reading each story to assess comprehension, reinforce early reading skills, and develop and practice oral and written language.

Before expecting students to work independently, read the directions for each activity and model appropriate responses. The Skills Chart on page 4 provides an overview of the skills practiced in the activities. The focus skills for each activity are printed at the bottom of the worksheet.

Skills Chart

Stories \ Skills	Letter/sound association	Predicting	Inferring	Classifying/categorizing	Rhyming words	Word families	Compound words	Following directions	Relating prior knowledge	Answering questions	Recalling story details	Critical thinking	Sequencing	Using context clues	Developing vocabulary	Word endings	Possessives	Pronouns	Comparative/Superlative	Using complete sentences	Organizing information
In My Bed	●					●		●			●			●							
Turn Off the TV		●			●					●	●	●		●	●						
Under an Umbrella						●		●		●	●	●		●	●						
Here Comes the Net	●			●		●		●			●										●
The Busy Pond	●				●			●			●	●									
Munch, Munch				●		●		●			●										
A Shortcut	●					●	●			●	●			●							
Getting Ready to Go		●		●		●		●			●				●						
I Have a Ticket			●	●			●		●		●	●			●						
Star Man					●	●		●		●	●	●								●	
What Will I Take?				●		●			●		●	●									●
Shake Pudding					●			●	●	●			●								
What Can You Put in It?	●					●	●	●			●										
Trucks			●	●				●			●				●	●					
The Campfire					●		●			●	●	●		●						●	
Ally's Garden					●						●	●	●	●	●					●	
Rainy Day Fun						●			●	●	●	●		●	●					●	
The Polar Bear						●		●	●	●	●	●		●		●				●	●
Moving Air						●		●	●	●	●	●		●							
Sam's Blue Hat										●	●		●				●		●	●	
Sparky					●		●				●						●				
It's Morning					●				●									●		●	
Hide-and-Seek	●							●	●	●	●			●	●					●	
Zack's Sandwich						●				●	●	●		●						●	●
The Pet Show									●		●				●			●			

Picture Dictionary Word List

In My Bed
bunny
blanket
book

Turn Off the TV
Mom
Gramps
Addy

Under an Umbrella
umbrella
man
dog

Here Comes the Net
net
big fish
little fish
baby fish

The Busy Pond
frogs
fish
ducks
bugs
children

Munch, Munch
goats
squirrels
children

A Shortcut
hilltop
butterfly
woodpile

Getting Ready to Go
black
white
striped
spotted
checkered

I Have a Ticket
ticket
football
movie
zoo

Star Man
star
window
milk
cookies

What Will I Take?
pajamas
toothbrush
teddy bear
pillow

Shake Pudding
cup
milk
lid
spoon

What Can You Put in It?
dragon
rocks
shoe
teacher

Trucks
horses
ladder
hose
blocks
toys

The Campfire
campfire
sounds
owl
sleeping bag

Ally's Garden
pulled
raked
planted
watered

Rainy Day Fun
splatter
sidewalk
branch
puddle

The Polar Bear
North Pole
swim
paddle
shake

Moving Air
move
push
sail
latch

Sam's Blue Hat
mouse
bunny
fox
ladybug

Sparky
nibble
kibble
snuggle

It's Morning
see
hear
touch
smell
taste

Hide-and-Seek
squirrel
turtle
insect

Zack's Sandwich
bread
pickle
ham
lettuce
sandwich

The Pet Show
tomorrow
bunny
carrots
kitten
fuzzy
puppy
happy

Picture Dictionary

bunny

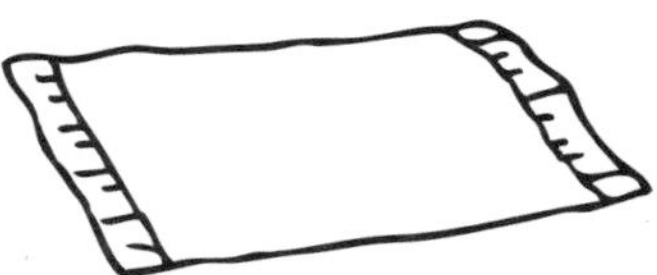

blanket

book

In My Bed

____
Name

1

I put my bunny in my bed.

2

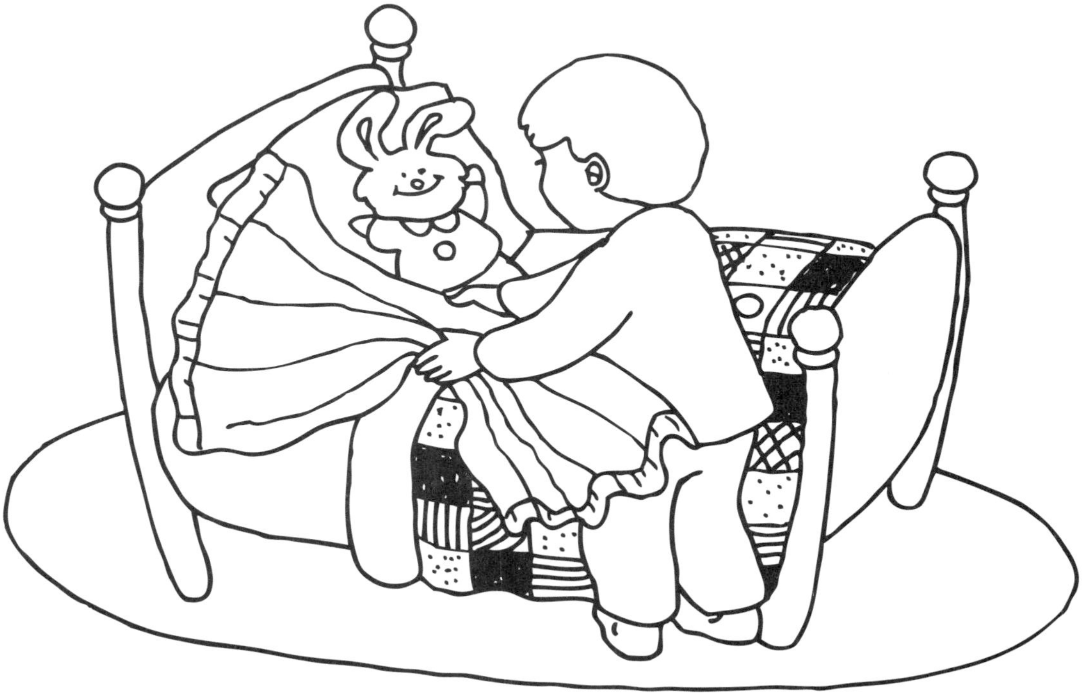

I put my blanket in my bed.

3

I put my book in my bed.
Is there room for me?

Name ______________________________

What Did the Story Say?

Draw the three things the boy put in his bed.

Draw what else needed to be in the bed.

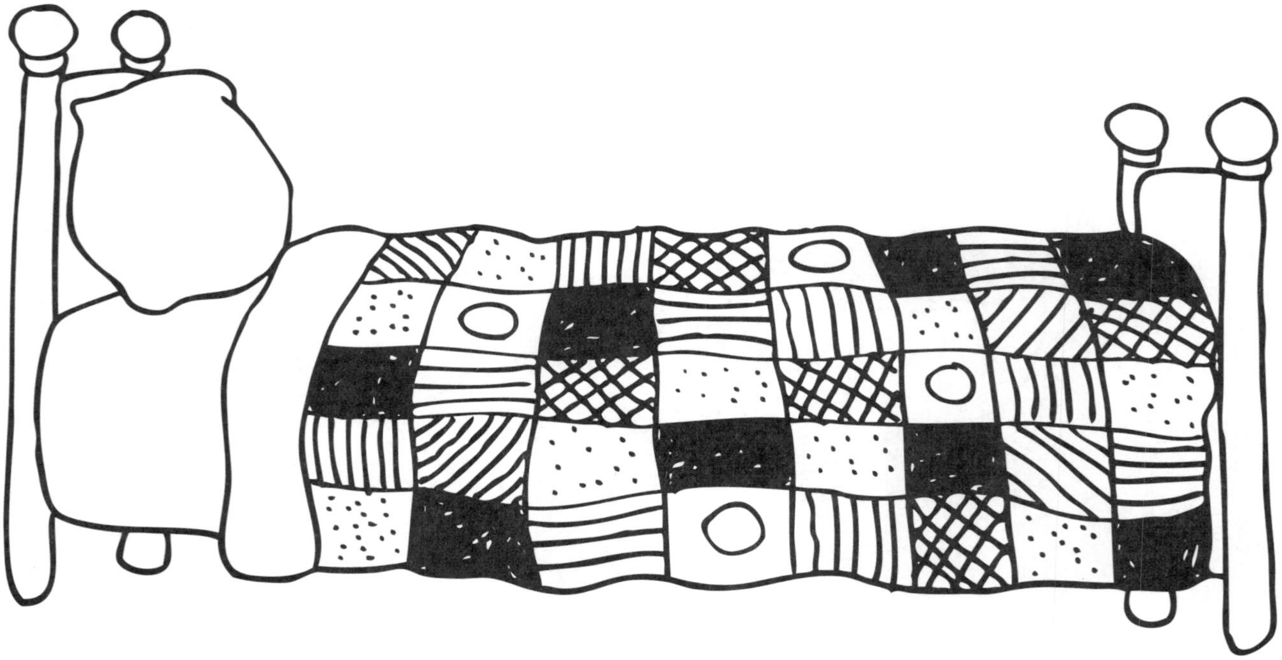

Name ______________________________

Working with Word Families

The **–un** word family can help you learn new words.
Write the words.

b + un = ___ ___ ___

s + un = ___ ___ ___

r + un = ___ ___ ___

f + un = ___ ___ ___

sp + un = ___ ___ ___ ___

Use the words to complete the sentences.

The ______________ is hot.

Put the hot dog on a ______________.

Going to the zoo is ______________.

My dog likes to ______________.

The spider has ______________ a web.

Skills: Read common word families **–un**; use context clues to complete sentences.

Name ____________________

Listen for the Sound.......... Bb

Color the pictures that begin with the /**b**/ sound.

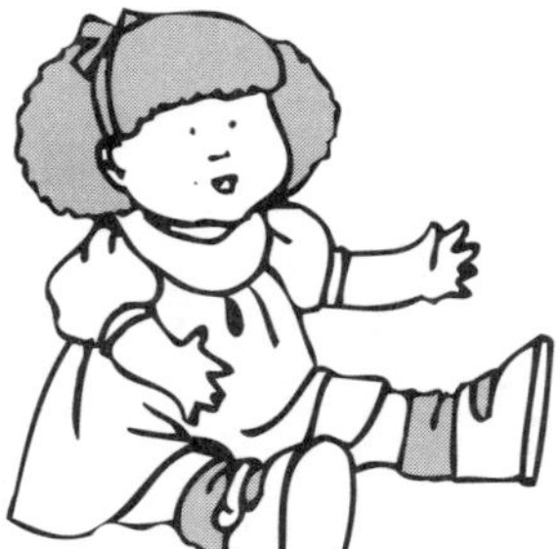
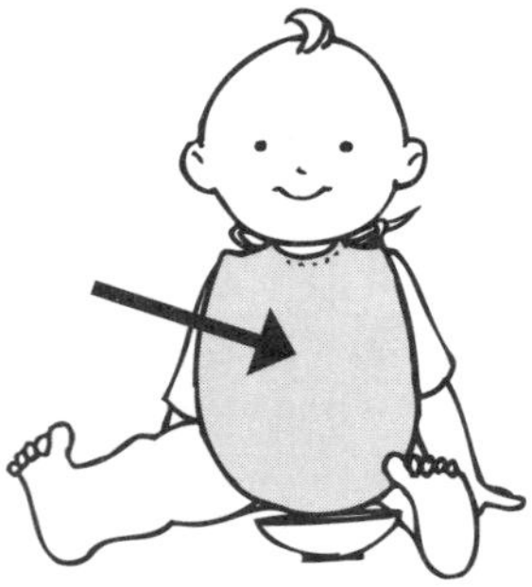
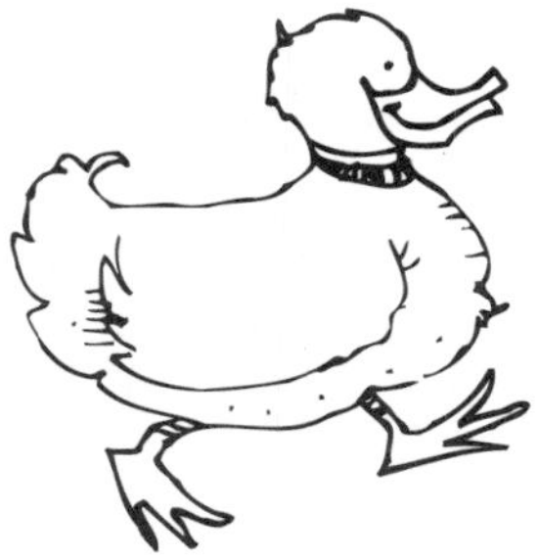
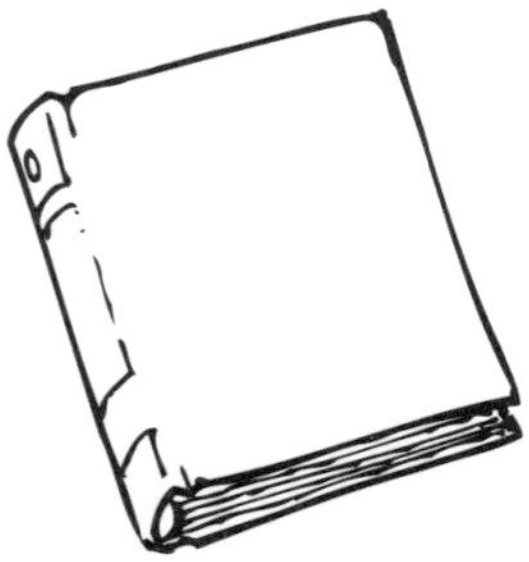
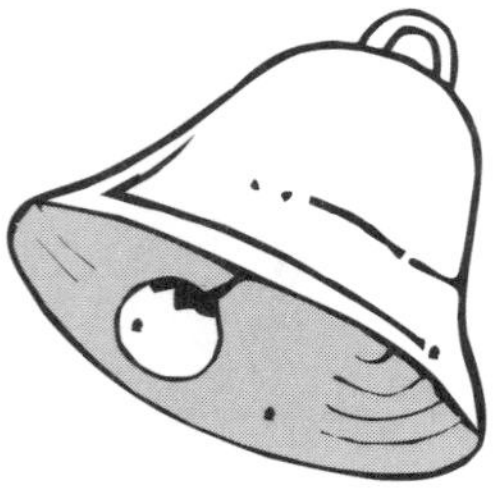
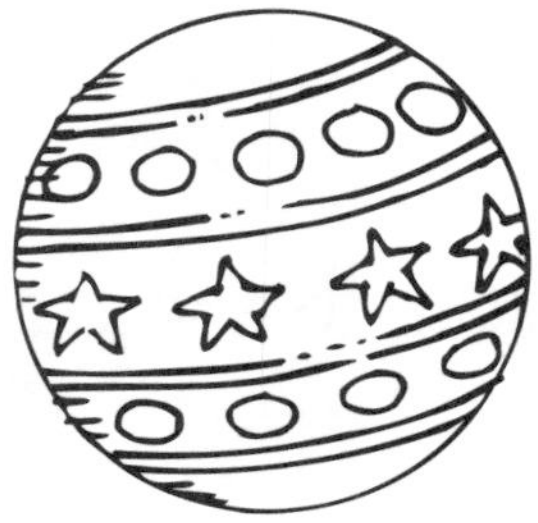
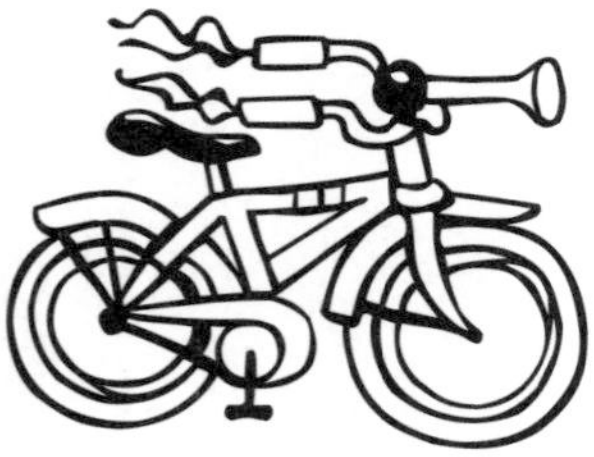
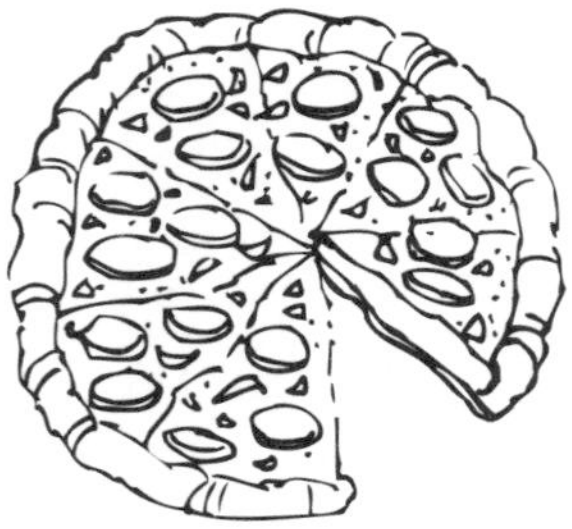
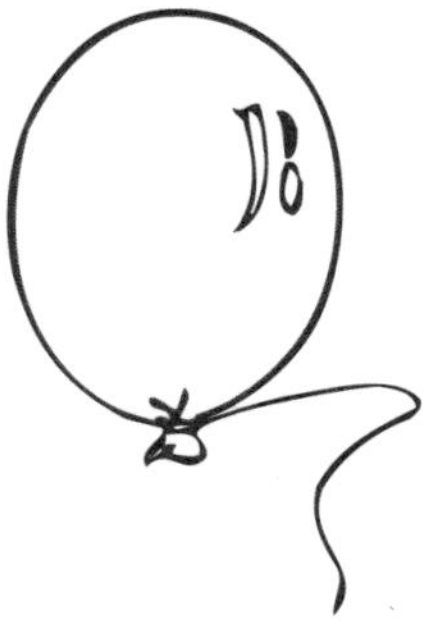
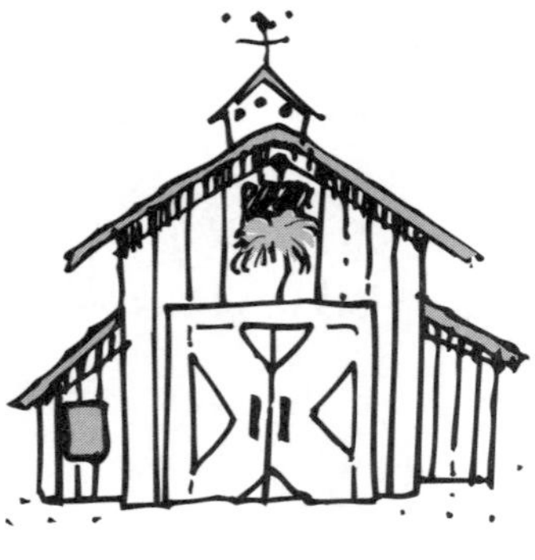
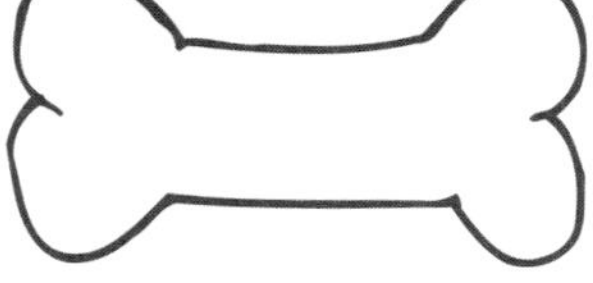
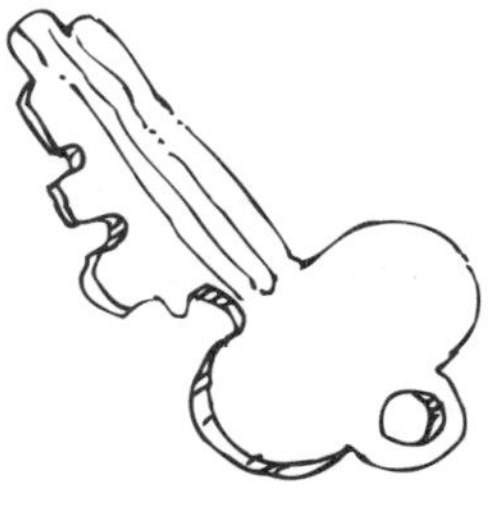

 Skill: Discriminate the letter **b** as an initial sound.

Name ______________________________

A Fun Place to Sleep

Connect the dots to draw a fun place to sleep.
Start with **1** and count to **25**.

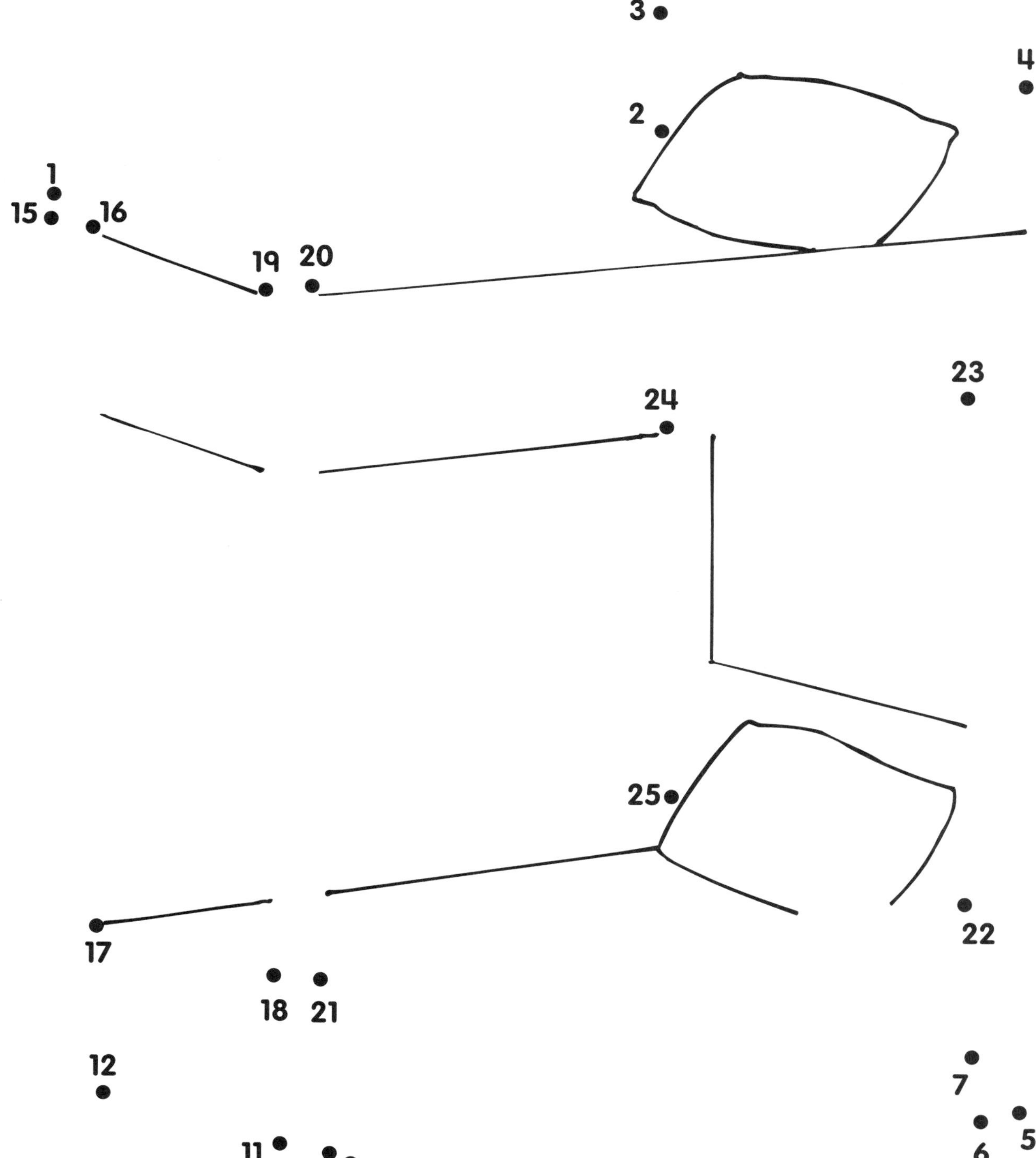

Skills: Follow directions; practice small motor skills.

Picture Dictionary

Mom

Gramps

Addy

Turn Off the TV

____

Name

1

Mom said, "Please turn off the TV."

2

Gramps said, "Please turn off the TV."

3

Addy said, "Please turn off the TV."

Name ________________________________

What Did the Story Say?

Circle to show that you remember what the story said.

What was Addy doing at the beginning of the story?

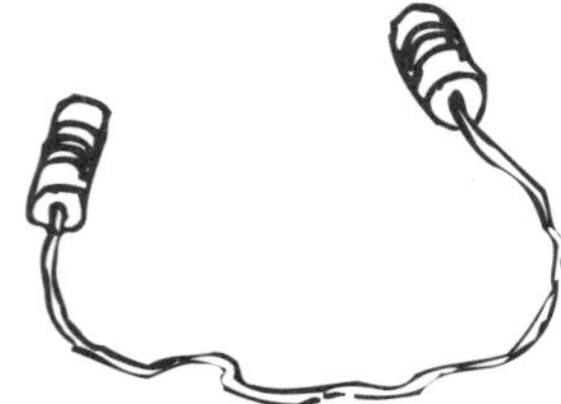

Who was watching TV at the end of the story?

Draw something Addy could do when the TV is off.

 Skills: Recall story details; answer *who* and *what* questions; predict future action; practice critical thinking.

Name ___________________________

Rhyme Time

Make an **X** on the things that rhyme with **please**.

Name ________________________________

On or Off?

Write **on** or **off** under each picture.

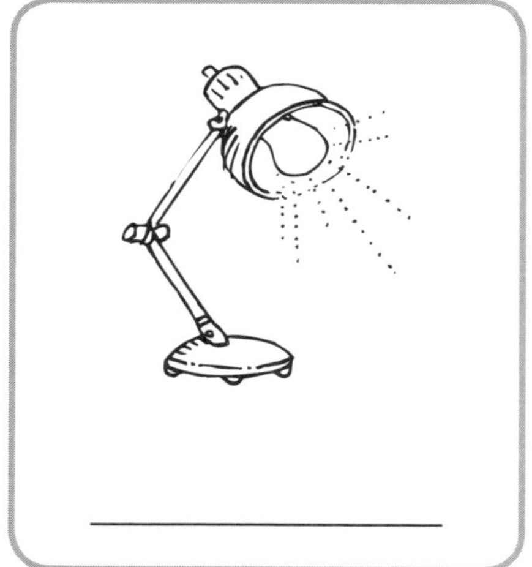

____

____

____

____

____

____

____

____

Skills: Practice word meaning; identify pictures by function.

Name ____________________

What Could You Do?

Draw four things that you could do at your house when the TV is off.

I could...

I could...

I could...

I could...

Skills: Practice critical thinking; prewriting activity.

Picture Dictionary

umbrella

man

dog

Under an Umbrella

____
Name

1

The man is under an umbrella.

2

The dog is under an umbrella.

3

The bunny is under an umbrella, too.

Name ______________________________

What Did the Story Say?

Draw lines to match what goes together.

• The dog is under an umbrella.

• The man is under an umbrella.

• The bunny is under an umbrella.

Draw yourself under an umbrella.

 Skills: Recall story details; follow directions; prewriting activity.

Name ______________________________

Working with Word Families

The **–og** word family can help you learn new words.
Write the words. Then answer the questions.

d + og = ___ ___ ___  Do you have a dog? yes no	fr + og = ___ ___ ___ ___  Do you have a frog? yes no
l + og = ___ ___ ___ 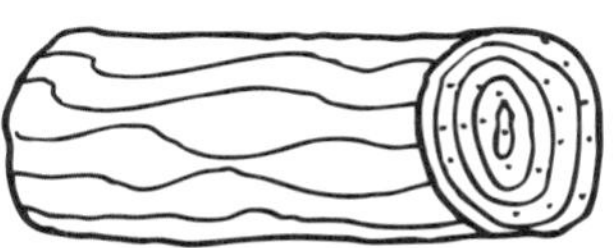 Can you jump over a log? yes no	f + og = ___ ___ ___  Can you see in the fog? yes no
j + og = ___ ___ ___  Do you like to jog? yes no	h + og = ___ ___ ___  Do you eat like a hog? yes no

Skills: Read common word families **–og**; answer *yes* or *no* questions; follow multi-step directions; practice critical thinking.

Name ______________________________

Words That Tell *Where*

Fill in the circle next to the words that tell *where* the bunny is.

O under the box
O on the box

O under the log
O on the log

O under the bed
O on the bed

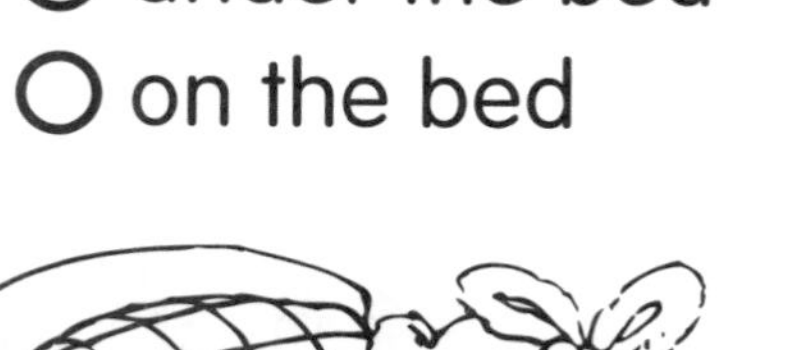

O under the pot
O on the pot

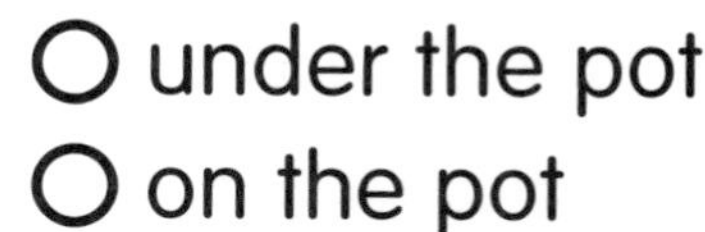

O under the wagon
O on the wagon

O under the chair
O on the chair

Skills: Use positional words; practice word meaning; use picture clues to strengthen comprehension.

Name ________________________________

Coloring Fun

Read the words to color the umbrella.
Then draw something under the umbrella.

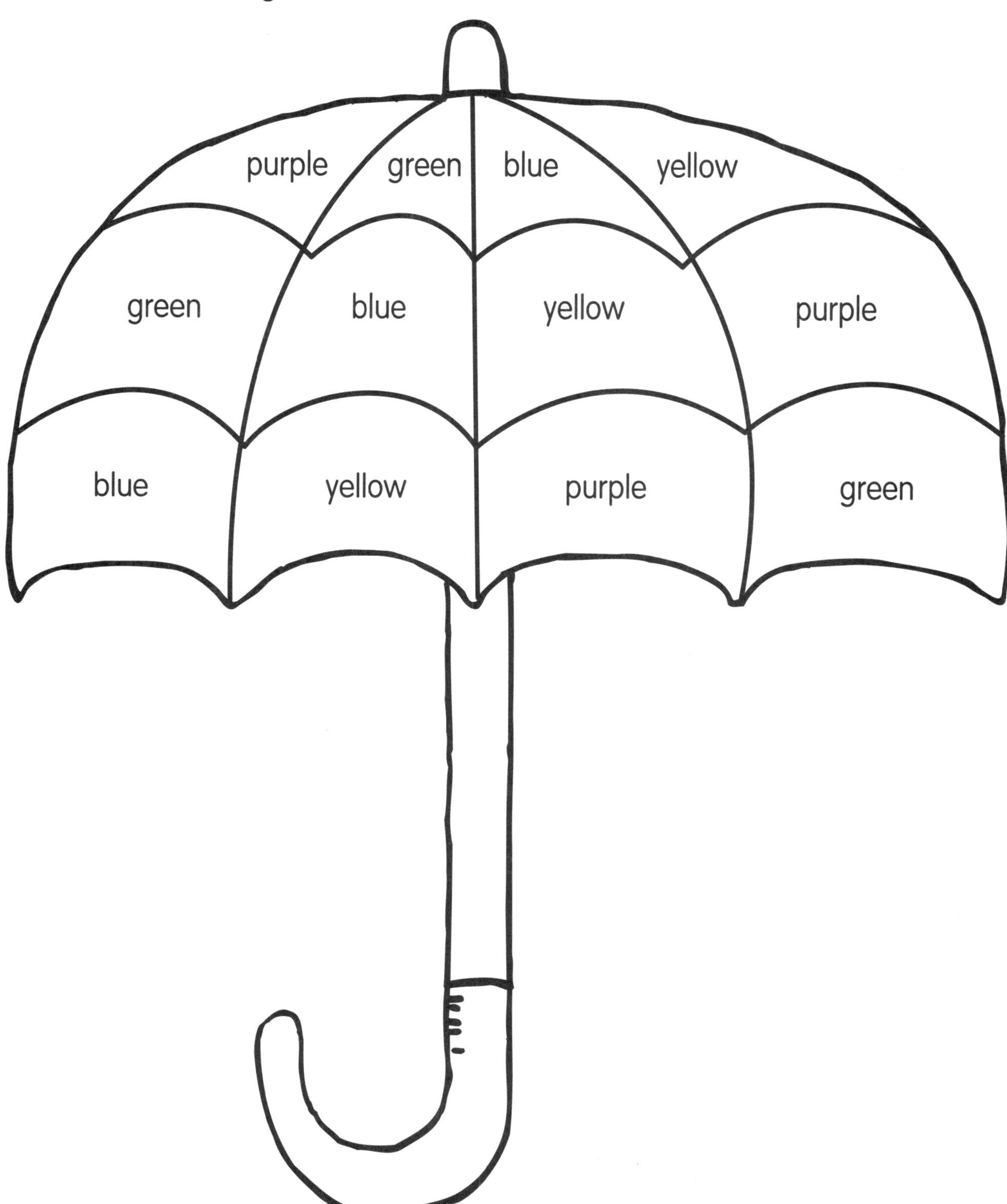

Skills: Read color words; follow multi-step directions.

Picture Dictionary

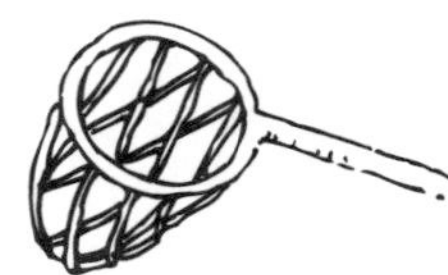

net

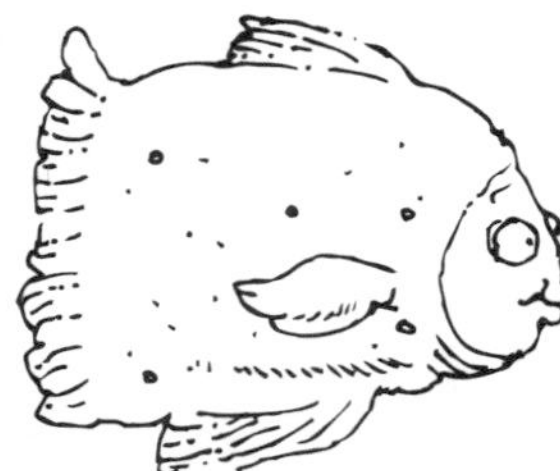

big fish

little fish

baby fish

Here Comes the Net

Name

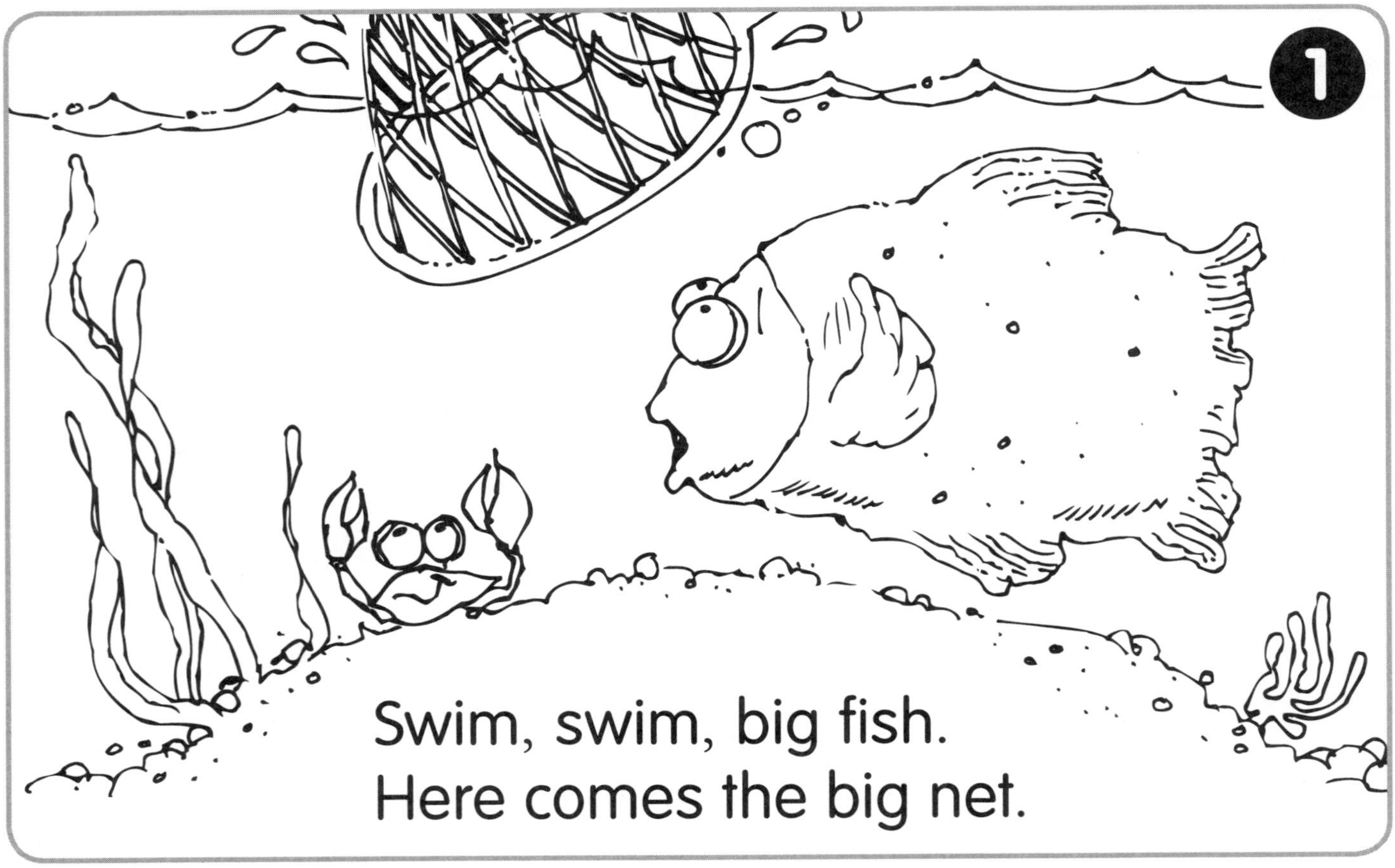

Swim, swim, big fish.
Here comes the big net.

2

Swim, swim, little fish.
Here comes the little net.

3

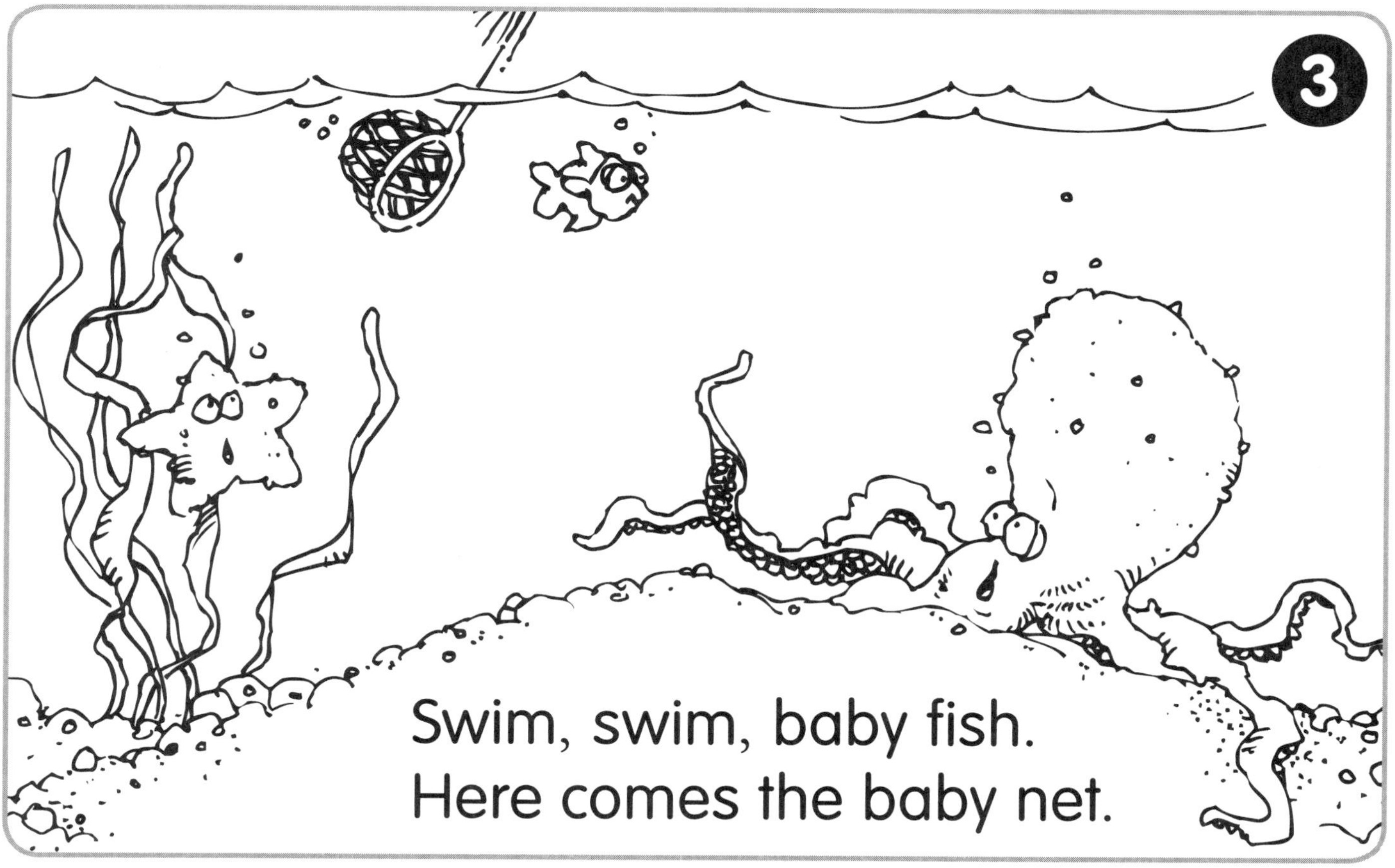

Swim, swim, baby fish.
Here comes the baby net.

Name ______________________________

What Did the Story Say?

Circle to show what happened in the story.

Which fish had to swim away from the big net?

big fish little fish baby fish

Which fish had to swim away from the little net?

big fish little fish baby fish

Which fish had to swim away from the baby net?

big fish little fish baby fish

 Skill: Recall story details.

Name ______________________________

Listen for the Sound........... sw

Color the pictures that begin with the /**sw**/ sound.

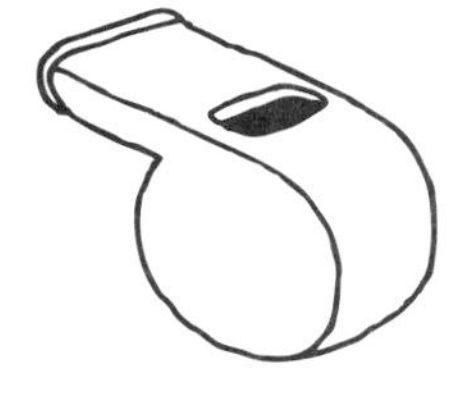

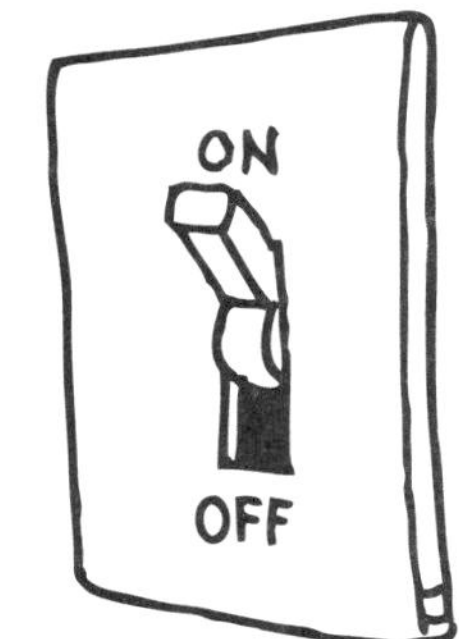

Skill: Discriminate the consonant blend **sw** as an initial sound.

Name ______________________________

Swim or Fly?

Cut and glue to put the animals into the correct groups.

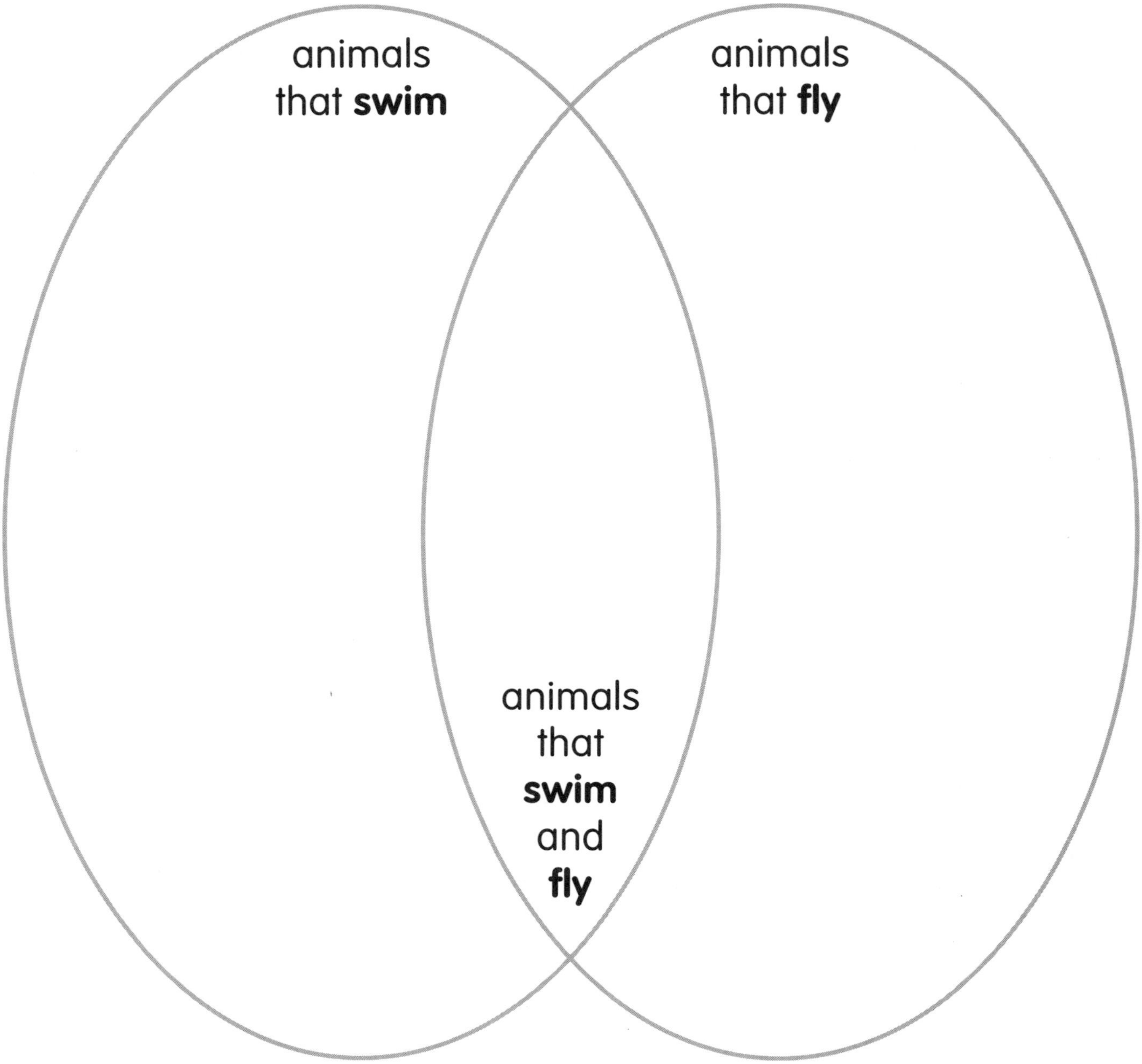

animals that **swim**

animals that **fly**

animals that **swim** and **fly**

 Skills: Use a graphic organizer to classify objects into categories; practice deductive reasoning.

Name ____________________

Working with Word Families

The **–ish** word family can help you learn new words. Write the words. Then draw the pictures.

f + ish = ___ ___ ___ ___ Draw a fish.	d + ish = ___ ___ ___ ___ Fill the dish. 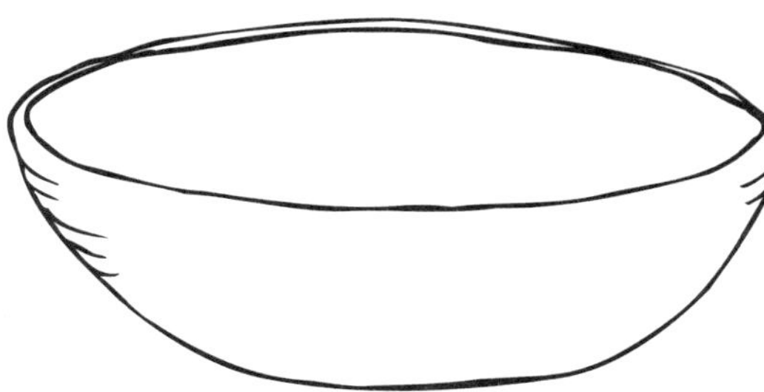
w + ish = ___ ___ ___ ___ Show your wish.	sw + ish = ___ ___ ___ ___ ___ What goes swish?

Skills: Read common word families **–ish**; follow multi-step directions.

Picture Dictionary

frogs

fish

ducks

bugs

children

The Busy Pond

Name

1

The pond is busy.
Frogs jump.
Fish swim.

2

Ducks quack.
Bugs fly.

3

Children play.
The pond is busy.

Name ________________________________

What Did the Story Say?

Color the things that made the pond busy.

Draw something else you might see at a pond.

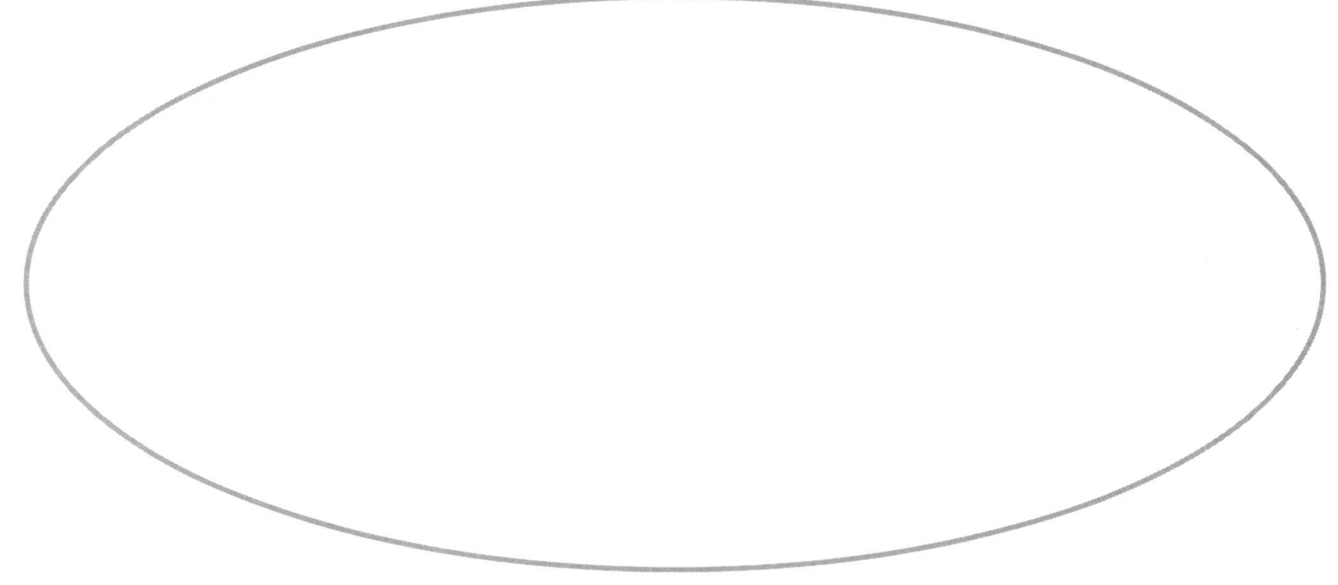

 Skills: Recall story details; practice critical thinking.

Name ______________________________

Rhyme Time

Color, cut, and glue to show rhyming pairs.

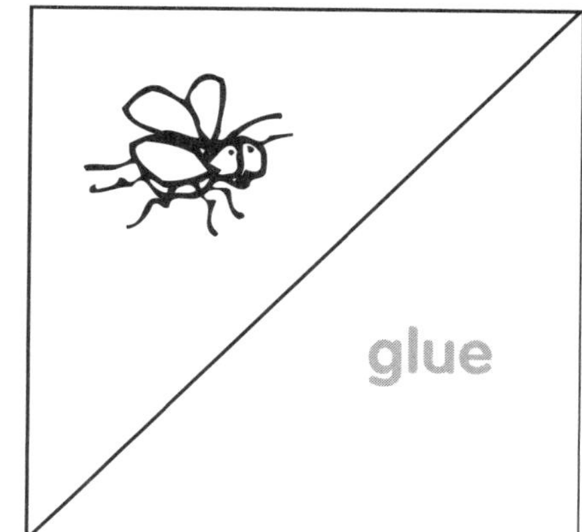

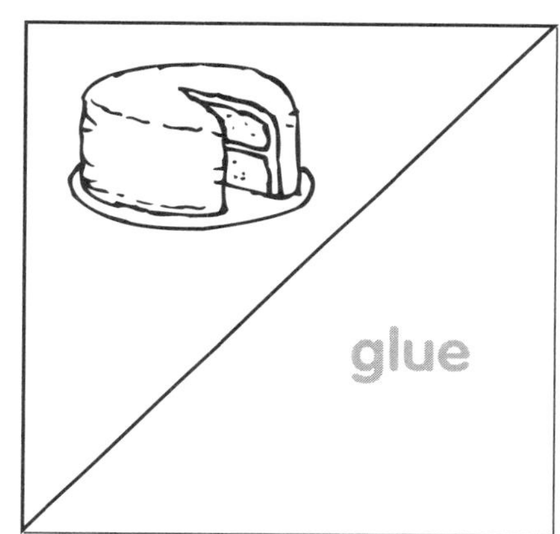

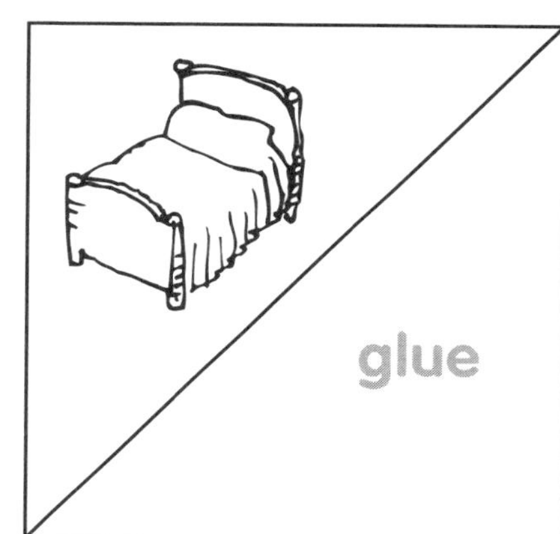

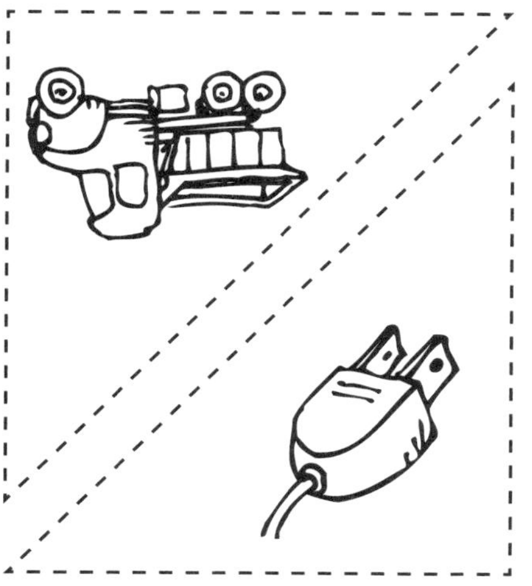

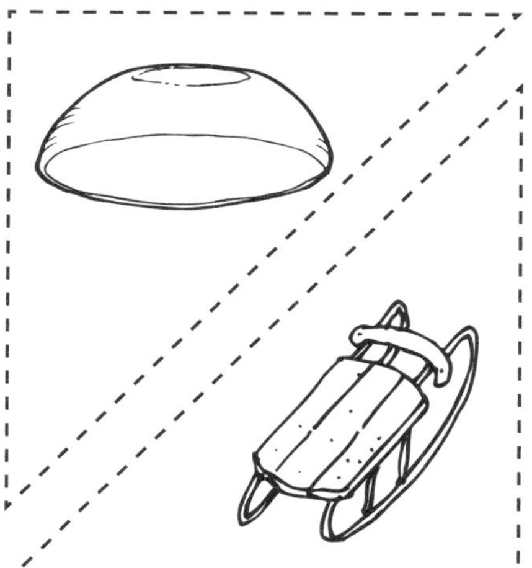

Skills: Identify rhyming words; follow multi-step directions.

Name ___________________________

Real or Make-Believe?

Circle **yes** or **no**.

A duck can quack.	A duck can fly.	A duck can read.
yes no	yes no	yes no
A frog can color.	A frog can jump.	A frog can swim.
yes no	yes no	yes no
A bug can hop.	A bug can paint.	A bug can race.
yes no	yes no	yes no

 Skills: Distinguish between real and make-believe; practice deductive reasoning.

Name ________________________________

Listen for the Sound.......... Pp

Color the pictures that begin with the /**p**/ sound.

Picture Dictionary

goats

squirrels

children

Munch, Munch

____

Name

See the goats.
They eat hay.
Munch, munch, good lunch.

2

See the squirrels.
They eat nuts.
Munch, munch, good lunch.

3

See the children.
They eat food.
Munch, munch, good lunch.

Name ____________________

What Did the Story Say?

Draw lines to show what they ate in the story.

squirrels •	• hay
goats •	• food
children •	• nuts

Draw a picture for this funny story about monkeys.

See the monkeys.
They eat a bunch.
Munch, munch, good lunch!

 Skills: Recall story details; use creative imagination; practice deductive reasoning.

Name ___________________________

Working with Word Families

The **–ay** word family can help you learn new words. Write the words. Then color, cut, and glue to show what each word means.

h + ay =	r + ay =	tr + ay =
___ ___ ___	___ ___ ___	___ ___ ___ ___
glue	glue	glue
cl + ay =	**spr + ay =**	**pl + ay =**
___ ___ ___ ___	___ ___ ___ ___ ___	___ ___ ___ ___
glue	glue	glue

Write two more **–ay** words. ______________ ______________

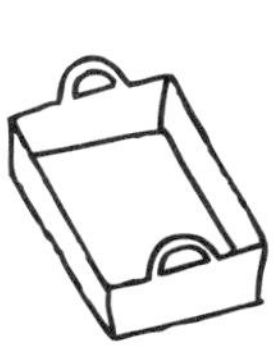

Skills: Read common word families **–ay**; follow multi-step directions; decode words with initial consonant blends.

Name ____________________

Does It Crunch?

Circle **yes** if the food crunches when you eat it.
Circle **no** if the food does not crunch.

 yes no	 yes no	 yes no
 yes no	 yes no	 yes no
Wheat yes no	yes no	yes no
 yes no	 yes no	 yes no

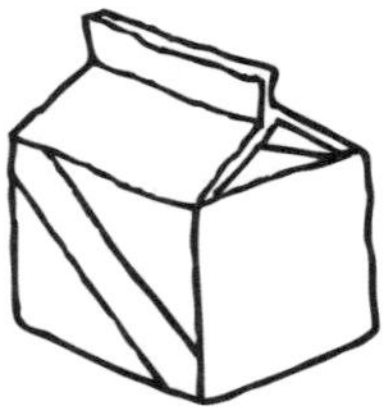

 Skill: Classify objects into categories.

Name ________________________________

My Favorite Lunch

Draw your favorite lunch.

Munch, munch, I eat ______________________ for lunch.

Picture Dictionary

hilltop

butterfly

woodpile

A Shortcut

Name

1

We must go home.
Let's race to the hilltop first.
Then we can take a shortcut.

2

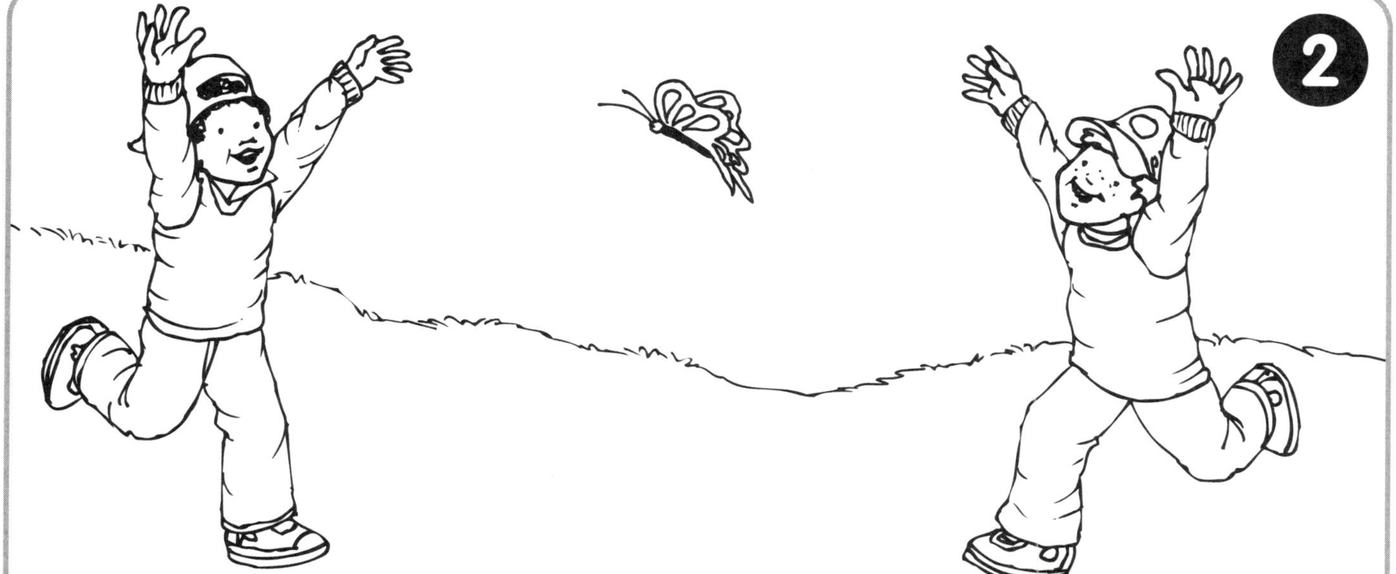

We must go home.
Let's catch a butterfly first.
Then we can take a shortcut.

3

We must go home.
Let's climb the woodpile first.
Then we will take a shortcut.

Name ____________________

What Did the Story Say?

Use the words in the box to answer the questions.

butterfly	race	hilltop
woodpile	home	shortcut

Where did the boys have to go?

____

What did the boys catch?

____

What did the boys climb?

____

Where did the boys race to?

____

 Skills: Recall story details; answer *what* and *where* questions.

Name ___________________________

Working with Word Families

The **–ake** word family can help you learn new words.
Write the words.

t + ake = ___ ___ ___ ___

c + ake = ___ ___ ___ ___

sn + ake = ___ ___ ___ ___ ___

r + ake = ___ ___ ___ ___

b + ake = ___ ___ ___ ___

l + ake = ___ ___ ___ ___

Use the words to complete the sentences.

Jake used a ______________ to pile up the leaves.

Please ______________ this letter to the mailbox.

Molly helped her mom ______________ a ______________.

A long green ______________ lives by the ______________.

Name ________________________________

Listen for the Sound........... sh

Color the pictures that begin with the /**sh**/ sound.

 Skill: Discriminate the consonant blend **sh** as an initial sound.

Name ______________________

Compound Words

Write the two words that make each compound word.

cupcake  ______________ + ______________

butterfly  ______________ + ______________

hilltop  ______________ + ______________

bathtub  ______________ + ______________

woodpile  ______________ + ______________

birdbath  ______________ + ______________

carwash  ______________ + ______________

Skill: Divide compound words into their original word forms.

Picture Dictionary

 black

 white

 striped

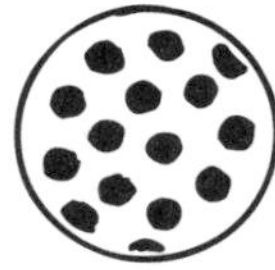 spotted

 checkered

Getting Ready to Go

Name

1

Black coat? No.
White coat? No.
Striped coat? Yes!

Are you ready to go? No!

2

White boots? No.
Black boots? No.
Spotted boots? Yes!

Are you ready to go? No!

3

Black hat? No.
White hat? No.
Checkered hat? Yes!

I am ready to go!

Name ______________________

Getting Ready to Go

What Did the Story Say?

Color the clothes to show what the girl picked.
Fill in the circle next to the word that tells about the clothes.

- O black
- O white
- O checkered
- O spotted
- O striped

- O black
- O white
- O checkered
- O spotted
- O striped

- O black
- O white
- O checkered
- O spotted
- O striped

 Skills: Recall story details; follow multi-step directions; develop vocabulary.

Name ______________________

Getting Ready to Go

Working with Word Families

The **–at** word family can help you learn new words.
Write the words. Then draw the pictures.

Draw a hat on a rat.

h + at = ___ ___ ___

r + at = ___ ___ ___

Draw a cat with a bat.

c + at = ___ ___ ___

b + at = ___ ___ ___

Draw something that is fat.

f + at = ___ ___ ___

Draw something that is flat.

fl + at = ___ ___ ___ ___

Skills: Read common word families **–at**; follow multi-step directions.

Name ____________________

Think and Draw

Show what might happen if your dad asked, “Are you ready to go?”

Show what might happen if your teacher asked, “Are you ready to go?”

Skill: Predict logical outcomes.

Name ______________________________

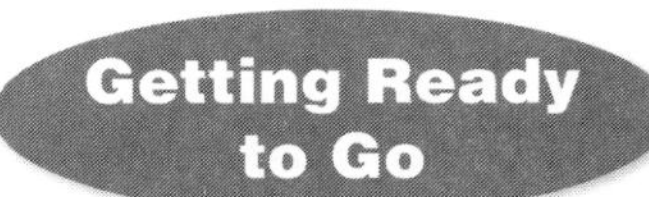

Match the Pairs

Match the pairs of socks and glue them in the correct boxes.

white socks		striped socks	
glue	glue	glue	glue

spotted socks		checkered socks	
glue	glue	glue	glue

Skill: Use visual discrimination to create matching sets.

Picture Dictionary

ticket

football

movie

zoo

I Have a Ticket

____
Name

1

I have a ticket.
I can go to a football game.
I can see the teams play.

2

I have a ticket.
I can go to a movie.
I can eat popcorn.

3

TICKETS

I have two tickets.
I can go to the zoo.
Will you come, too?

Name ______________________________

What Did the Story Say?

Answer the questions to tell what the story said.

Where did the first boy go?

____

Where did the girl go?

____

Where did the last boy go?

____

Would you like to go to the zoo?

____

Draw a place where you would need to have a ticket.

Skills: Recall story details; practice critical thinking; prewriting activity.

Name ______________________________

Where Would You Find It?

Cut and glue to show where you would find each thing.

at a football game	glue	glue
at a movie	glue	glue
at the zoo	glue	glue

Circle the one that you might find at all three places.

Skills: Classify objects into categories; infer common characteristics; relate prior knowledge to text.

Name ______________________________

Compound Words

Read the words in each row. Circle the compound word.

ticket	movie	popcorn
kicking	football	running
cupcake	candle	party
funny	bathtub	monkey
purple	happy	butterfly

Use the words in the box to make compound words.

cow	ball	boy
base	day	birth

1. ______________________________

2. ______________________________

3. ______________________________

 Skill: Identify and create compound words.

Name ______________________________

At the Zoo

Cut and glue to put the animals in their cages.

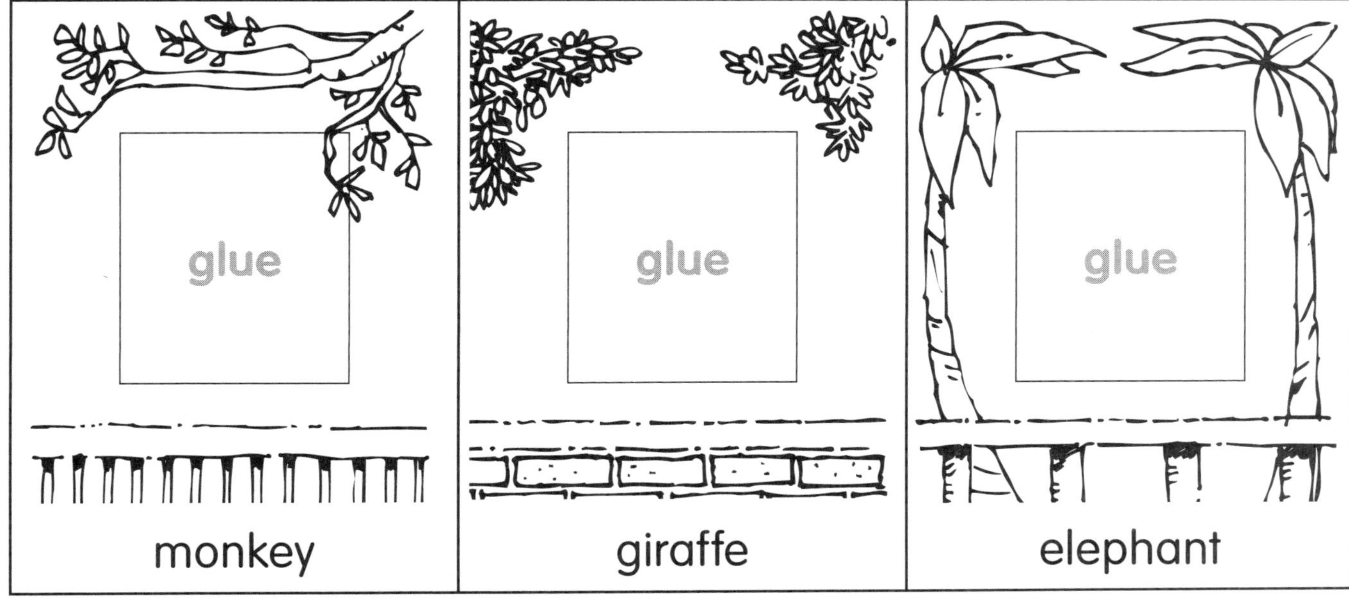

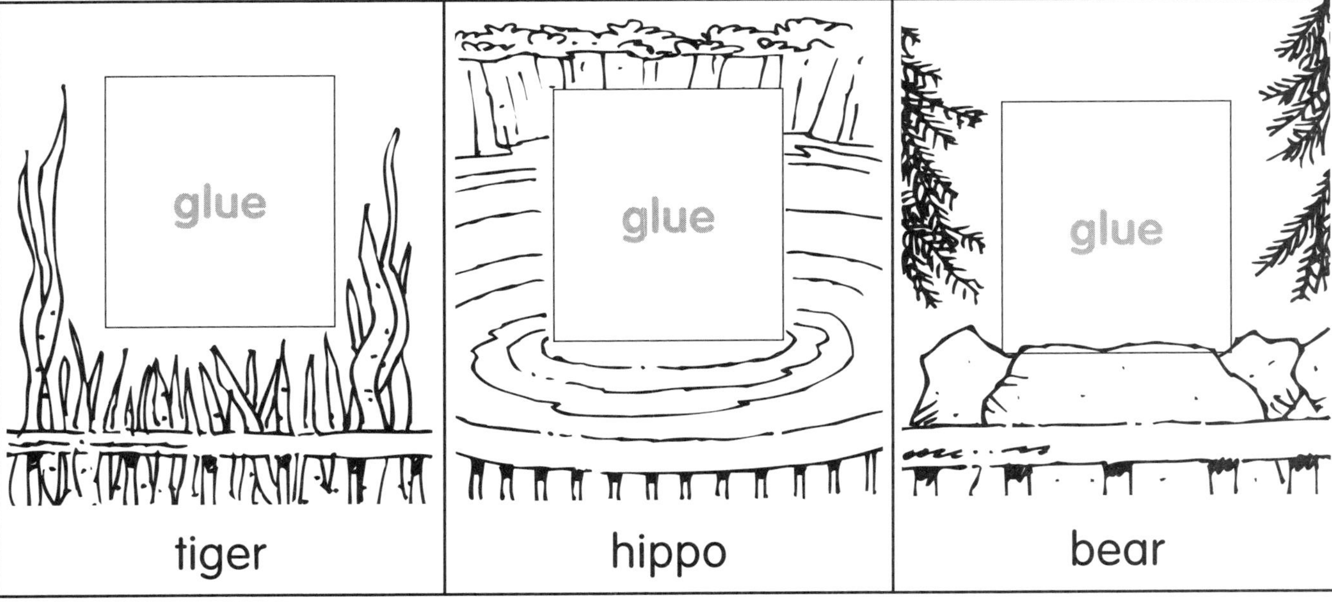

Skills: Develop vocabulary; relate prior knowledge to text.

Picture Dictionary

star

window

milk

cookies

Star Man

Name

1

Hello, Star Man.
I see you from my window.
I wonder about you.

2

Do you have a bed?
Do you like milk and cookies?
Do you go to sleep?

3

I see you in the sky.
I'm glad you stopped by.
Good night, Star Man.

Name ______________________________

What Did the Story Say?

What questions did the boy ask Star Man?

1. ______________________________

2. ______________________________

3. ______________________________

What questions would you ask Star Man?

1. ______________________________

2. ______________________________

3. ______________________________

Draw Star Man in the window.

 Skills: Recall story details; practice critical thinking; use creative imagination.

Name ______________________________

Working with Word Families

The **–ed** word family can help you learn new words.
Write the words. Then draw the pictures.

Draw Fred sleeping in his bed.

b + ed = ___ ___ ___

Fr + ed = ___ ___ ___ ___

Draw Ted on a red sled.

T + ed = ___ ___ ___

r + ed = ___ ___ ___

sl + ed = ___ ___ ___ ___

Draw Ned painting a shed.

N + ed = ___ ___ ___

sh + ed = ___ ___ ___ ___

Skills: Read common word families **–ed**; follow multi-step directions.

Name ______________________________

Rhyme Time

Circle the pictures that rhyme in each row.

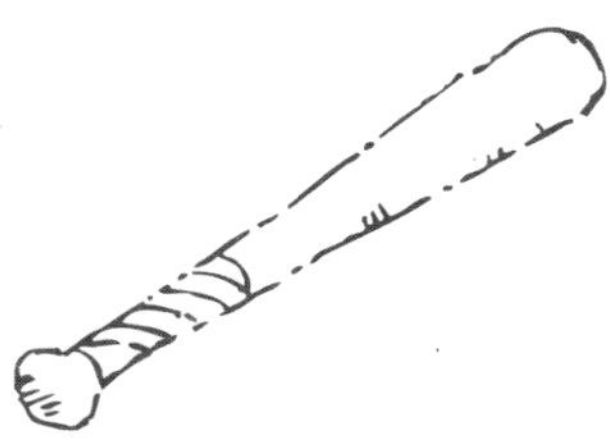

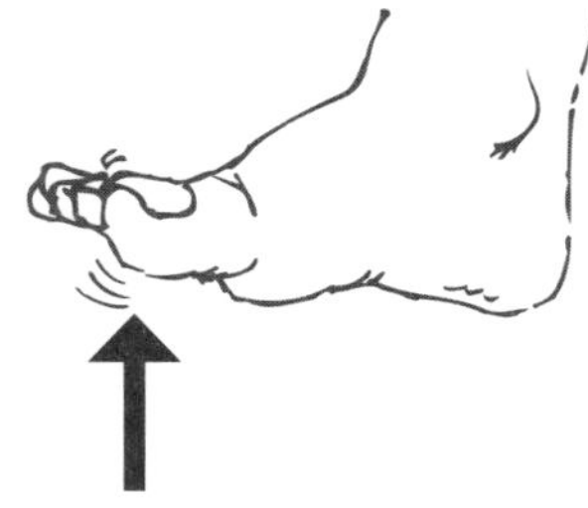

Name ________________________________

Questions and Answers

Write a sentence to answer each question.

Do you have a dog?

____

Do you like pizza?

____

Do you eat apples?

____

Do you play baseball?

____

Write a question. Then have a friend write the answer.

Question: ______________________________________

____

Answer: ____

____

Skills: Write complete sentences to answer questions; practice critical thinking.

Picture Dictionary

pajamas

toothbrush

teddy bear

pillow

What Will I Take?

Name

1

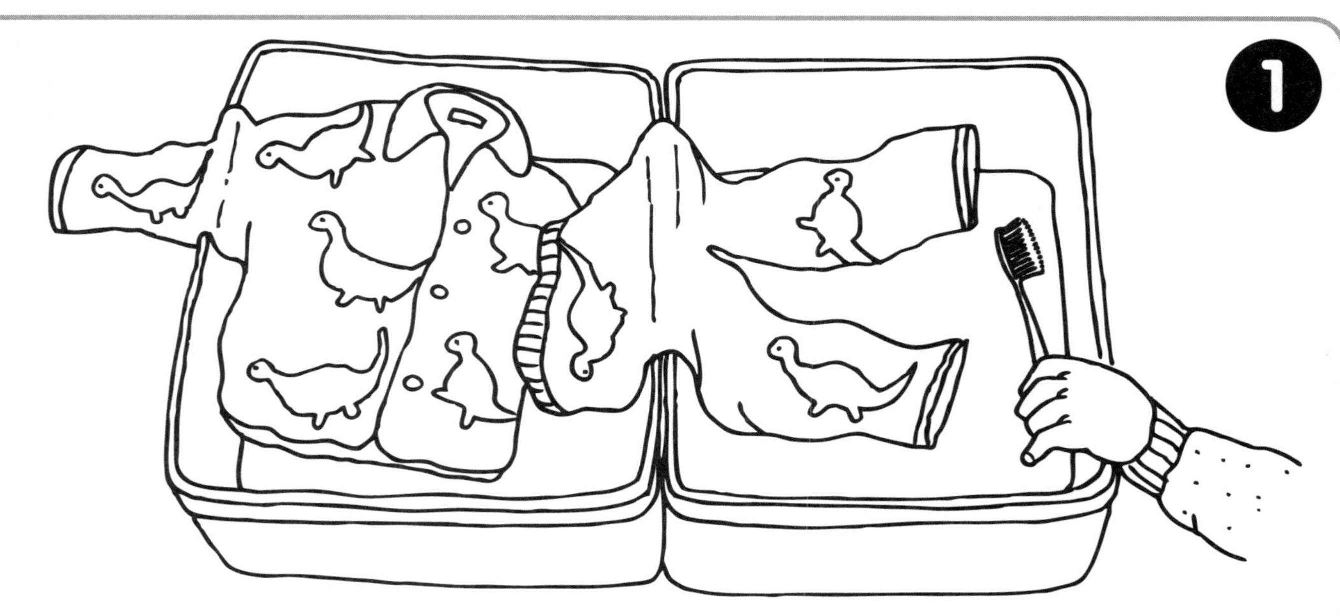

I am staying overnight at Grandma's.
I will take my pajamas.
I will take my toothbrush.

2

I will take my blue blanket.
I will take my teddy bear.
I will take my red socks.

3

I will take my book.
I will take my pillow.
I'm staying overnight at Grandma's.

Name ____________________

What Did the Story Say?

Cut and glue to show what the girl put into her suitcase.

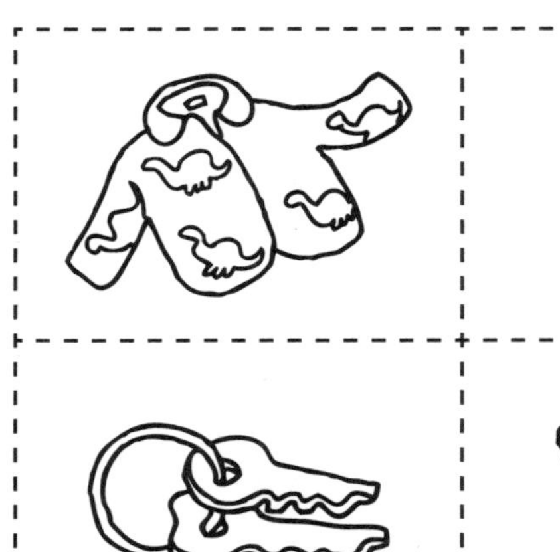

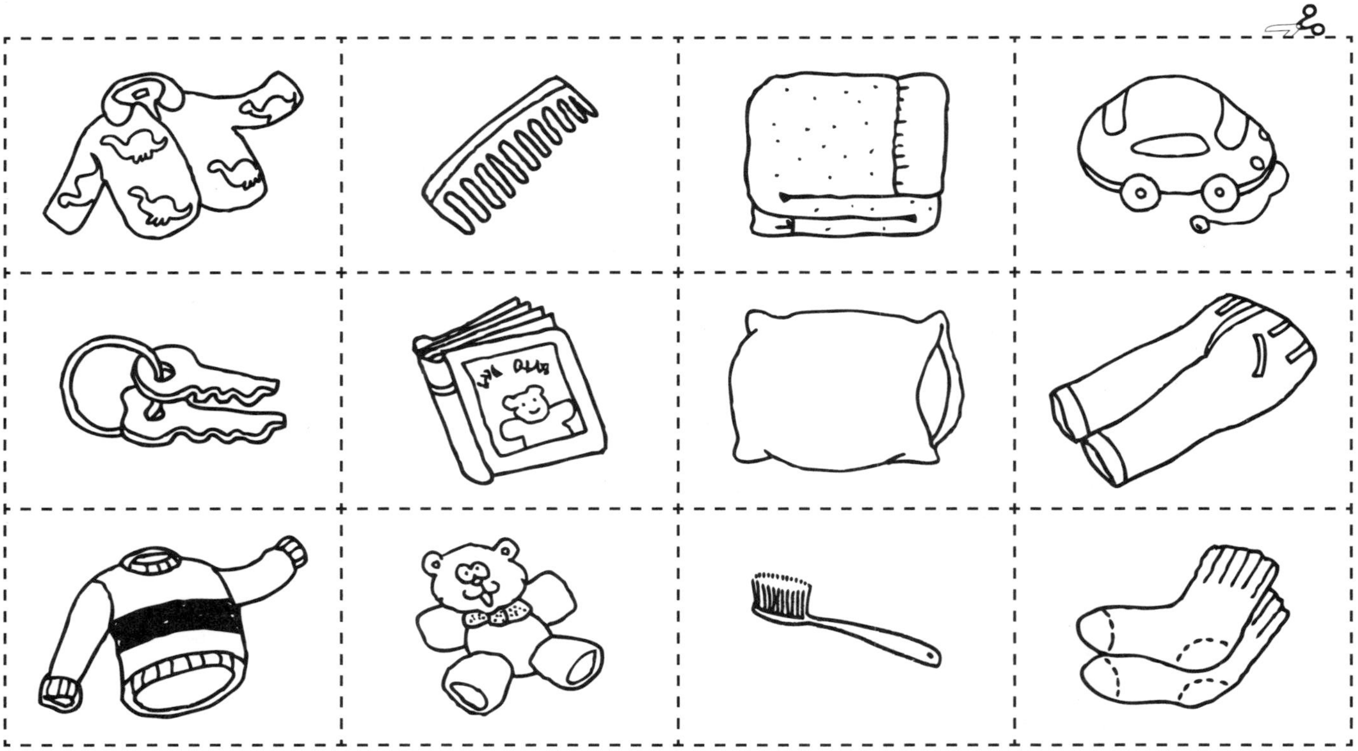

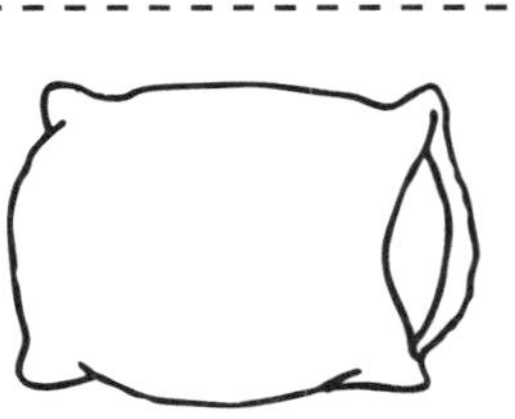

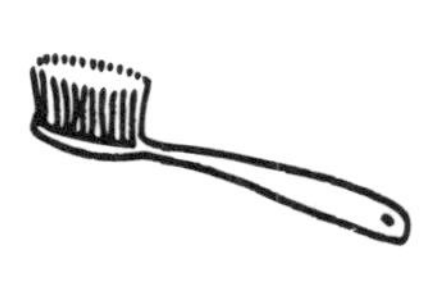

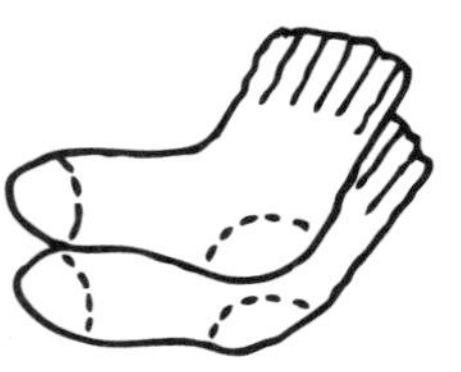

 Skill: Recall story details.

Name ______________________________

Working with Word Families

The **–ock** word family can help you learn new words. Write the words.

s + ock = ____ ____ ____ ____

d + ock = ____ ____ ____ ____

l + ock = ____ ____ ____ ____

r + ock = ____ ____ ____ ____

cl + ock = ____ ____ ____ ____ ____

bl + ock = ____ ____ ____ ____ ____

Write the word for each picture.

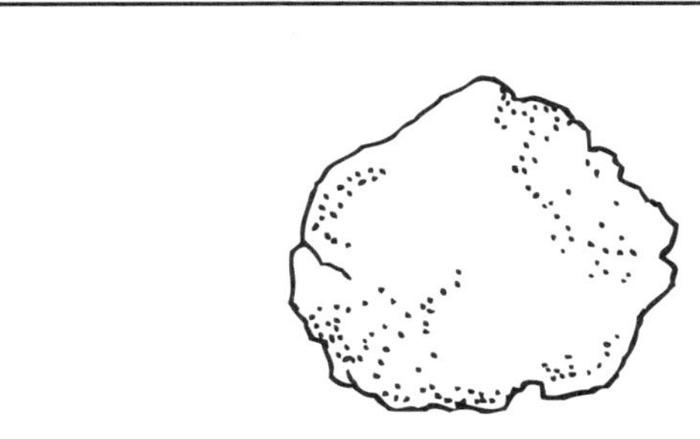 ____ ____ ____ ____	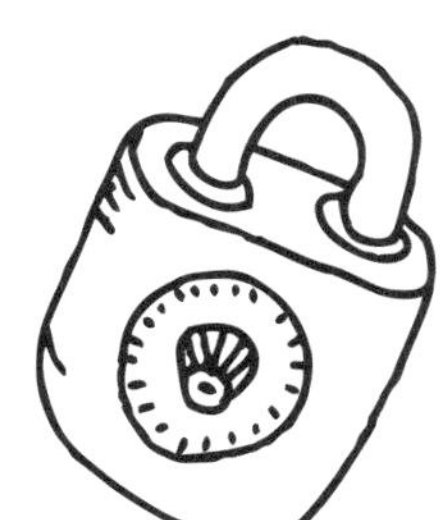 ____ ____ ____ ____
 ____ ____ ____ ____ ____	 ____ ____ ____ ____ ____

Name ________________________________

Hard or Soft?

Cut and glue to put the objects into the correct groups.

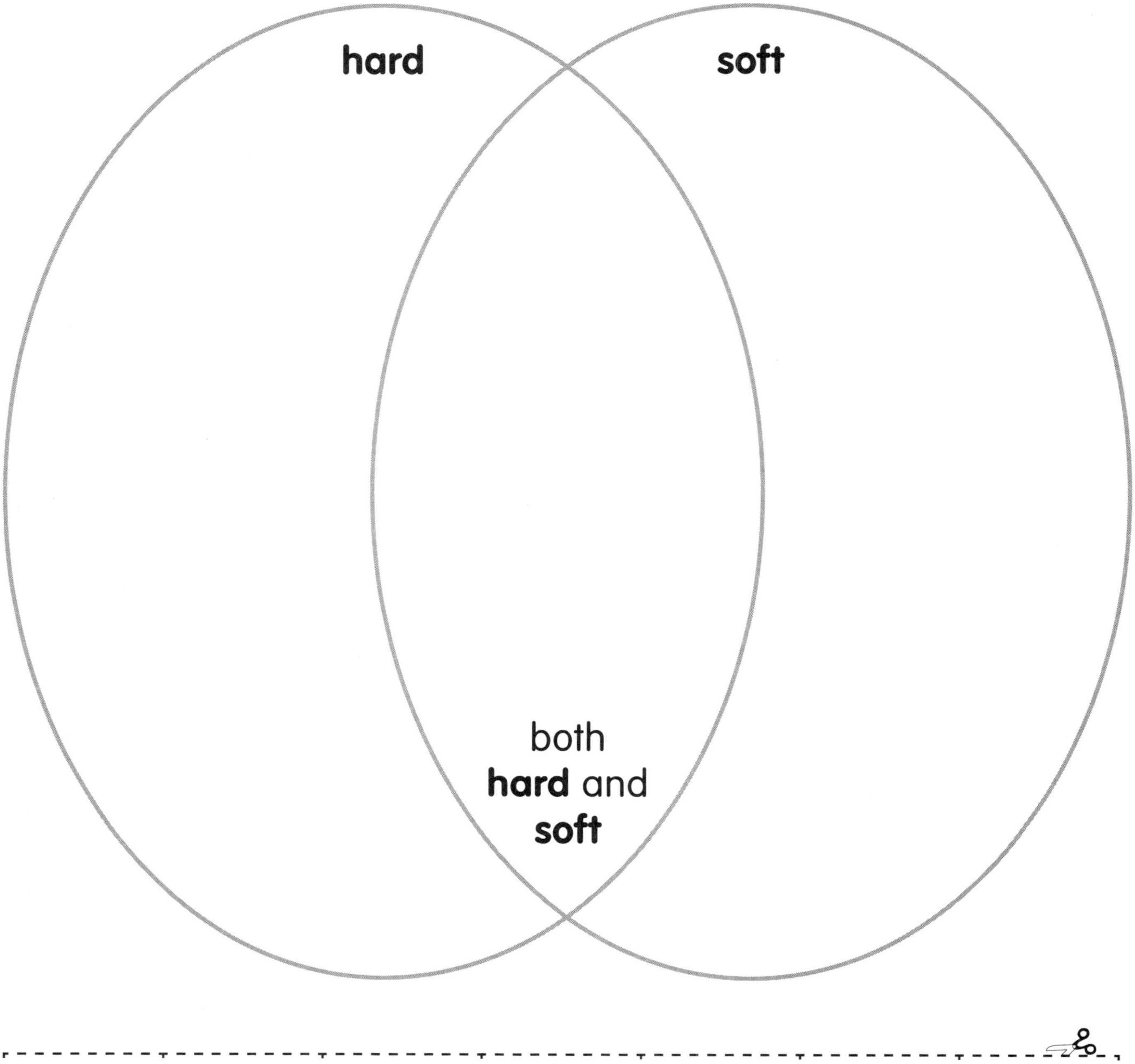

hard

soft

both **hard** and **soft**

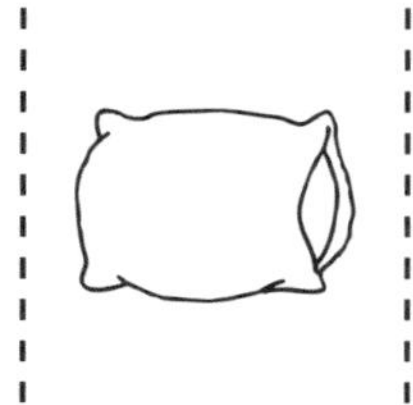

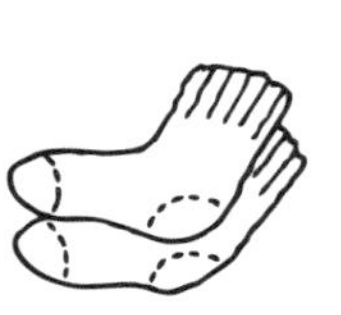

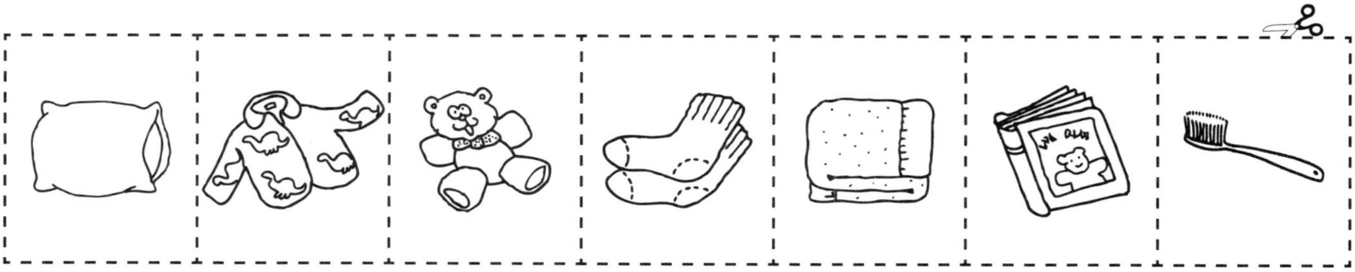

 Skill: Use a graphic organizer to classify objects into categories.

Name ______________________________

My Suitcase

Draw what you would pack in your suitcase if you were going away overnight.

Skills: Practice critical thinking; relate personal experience to text.

Picture Dictionary

cup

milk

lid

spoon

Shake Pudding

Name

1

Get a cup.
Put in the pudding.
Add some milk.

Mix it up.
Mix it up.
Mix it up fast.

2

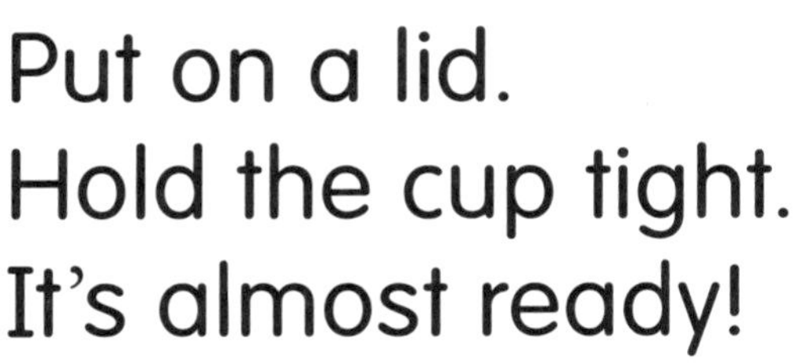

Put on a lid.
Hold the cup tight.
It's almost ready!

Shake it up.
Shake it up.
Shake it up fast.

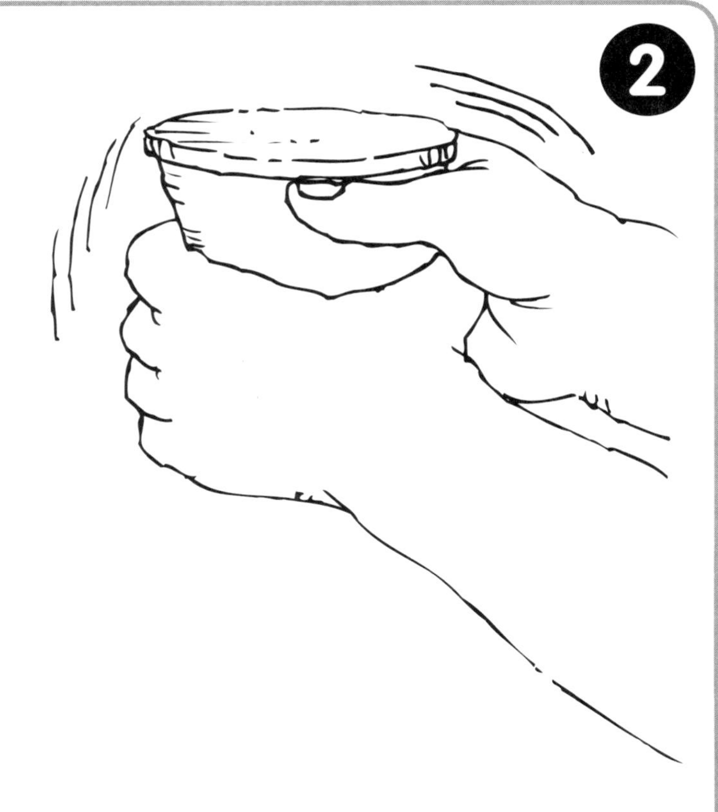

3

Now stop.
Take off the lid.
Get a spoon.

Eat it up.
Eat it up.
Eat it up fast.

Name ______________________

What Did the Story Say?

Cut and glue to put the steps in order.

1.	glue	2.	glue
3.	glue	4.	glue
5.	glue	6.	glue

Eat it up.	Get a cup.
Mix pudding and milk.	Shake it up.
Take off the lid.	Put on a lid.

 Skill: Sequence text to retell a story.

Name ______________________

Will You Eat It?

Write **yes** or **no** to tell if you will eat it.

Your mom says, "Eat it up fast."

Will you eat it? ____________

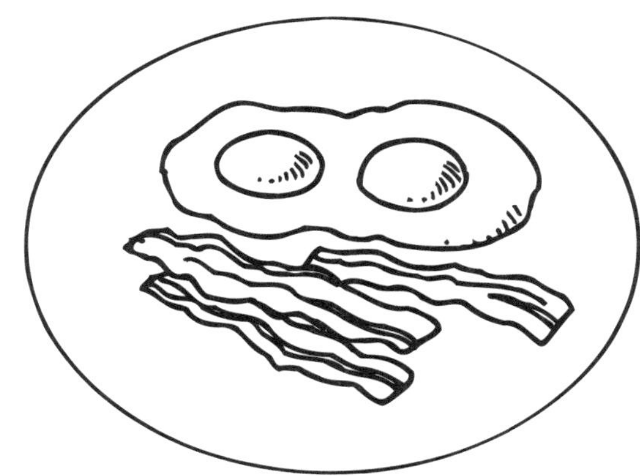

Your dad says, "Eat it up fast."

Will you eat it? ____________

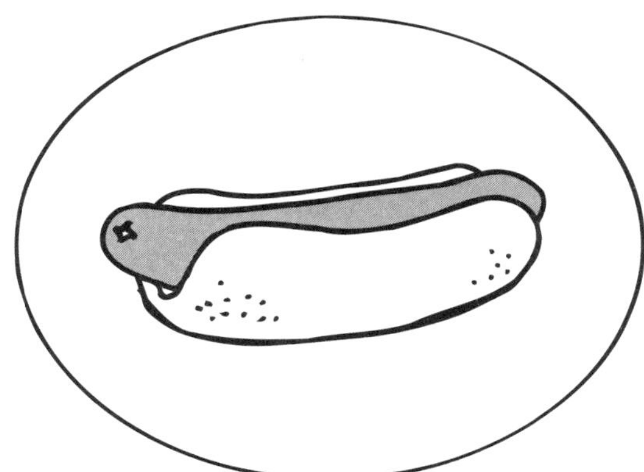

Your brother says, "Eat it up fast."

Will you eat it? ____________

Skills: Answer *yes* or *no* questions; relate personal experience to text.

Name ________________________________

Rhyme Time

Match the words that rhyme.

cup •	• hid
get •	• neat
tight •	• fix
mix •	• pup
shake •	• take
lid •	• last
fast •	• might
eat •	• wet

Circle the rhyming words in each sentence.

I bet I can get you wet!

The dog jumped over a log.

Will you run up the hill with Jill?

Name ______________________________

A Yummy Surprise

Connect the dots to draw a yummy surprise.
Start with **5** and count by fives to **100**.

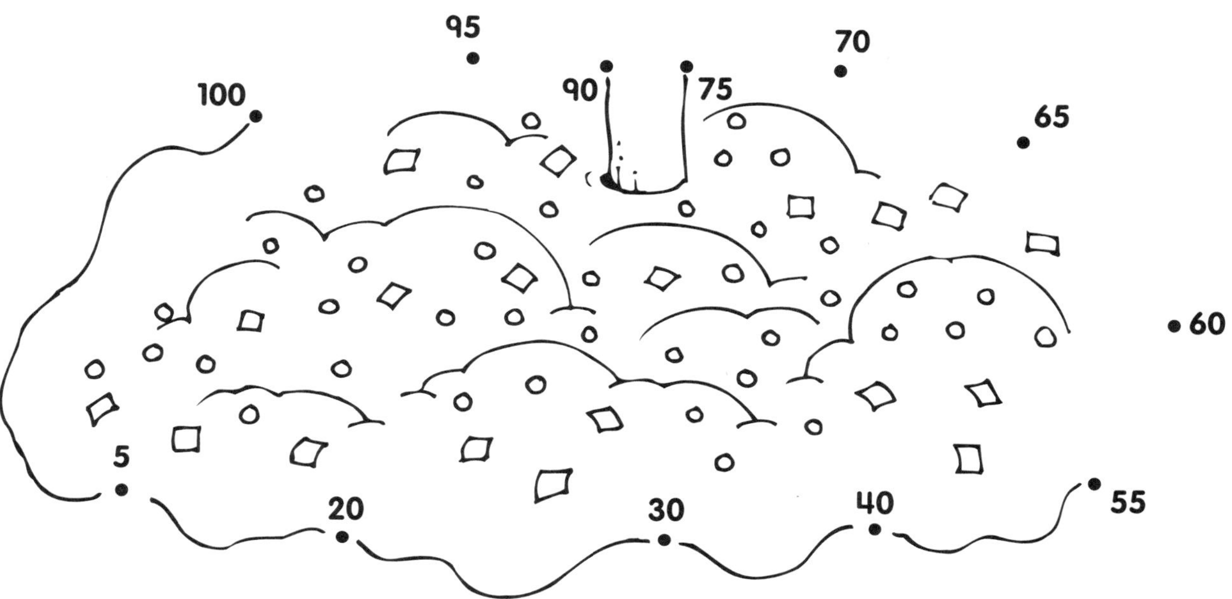

Will you eat it up fast? ________________

Picture Dictionary

dragon

rocks

shoe

teacher

What Can You Put in It?

Name

1

What can you put in a wagon?
A bag, a box, and a fuzzy dragon.

2

What can you put in a toy truck?
Some rocks, a shoe, and a yellow duck.

3

What can you put in a bus?
Our books, our teacher, and all of us.

Name ______________________

What Did the Story Say?

Write to tell what went in each one.

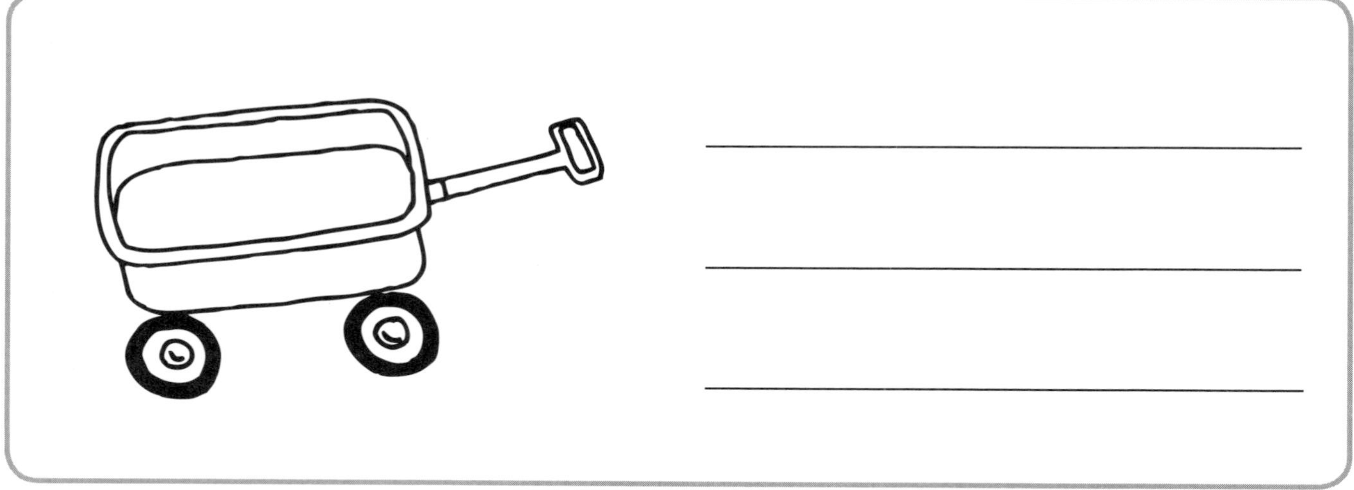

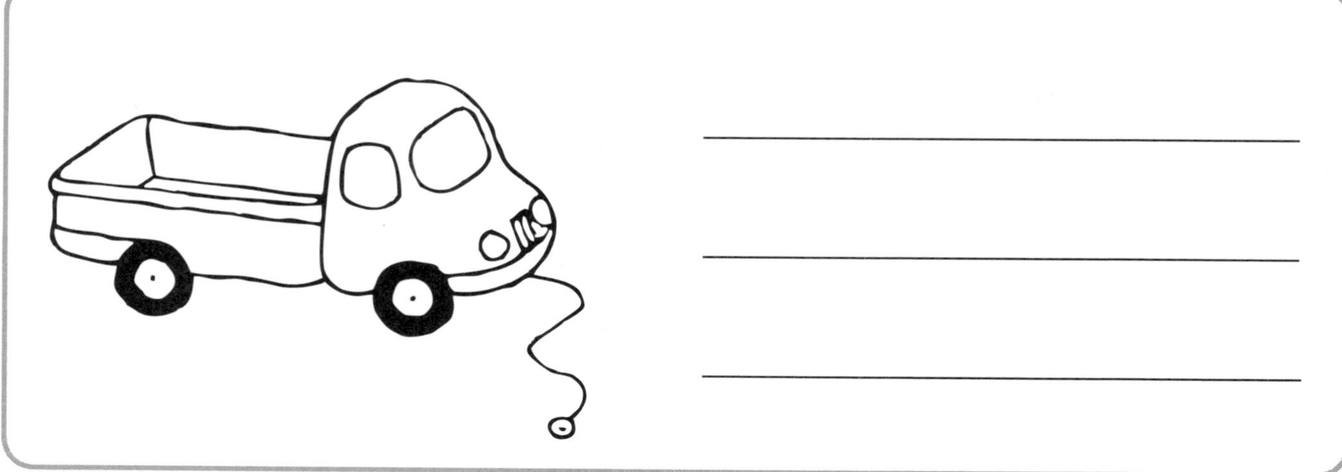

 Skill: Recall story details.

Name ______________________

Working with Word Families

The **–ag** word family can help you learn new words. Write the words.

b + ag = ___ ___ ___

t + ag = ___ ___ ___

r + ag = ___ ___ ___

fl + ag = ___ ___ ___ ___

dr + ag = ___ ___ ___ ___

z + ag = ___ ___ ___

Use the words to make compound words.

Tom threw his bean__________ and won the game.

Our school has a tall __________pole.

Clean the plate with the dish__________.

Draw a zig__________ on your paper.

Name ____________________

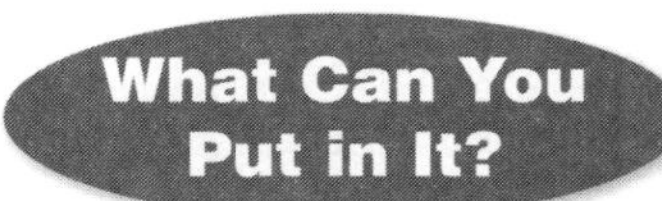

What's at the End?

Write the letter that stands for the sound you hear at the end of each word.

 ba___	 boo___
 bu___	 ma___
 cu___	 do___
 ca___	 ja___
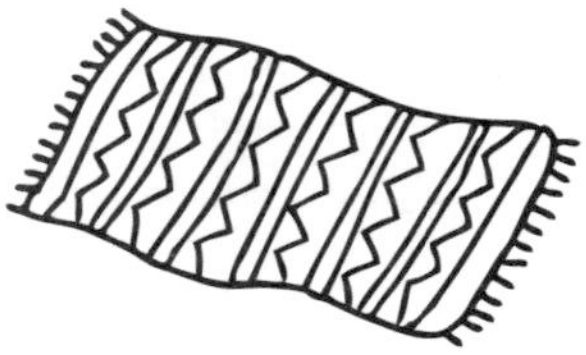 ru___	 tu___
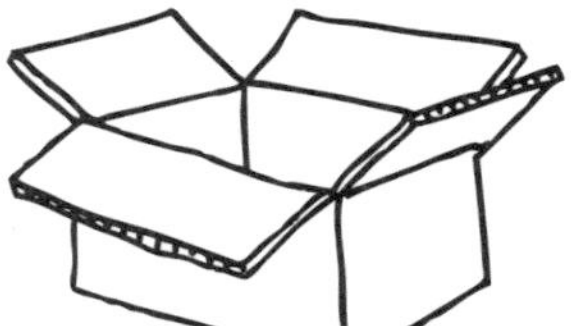 bo___	 boa___

 Skill: Discriminate final consonant sounds.

Name ____________________

Make a Wagon

Color, cut, and glue to make a wagon.
Then tell what you would put in it.

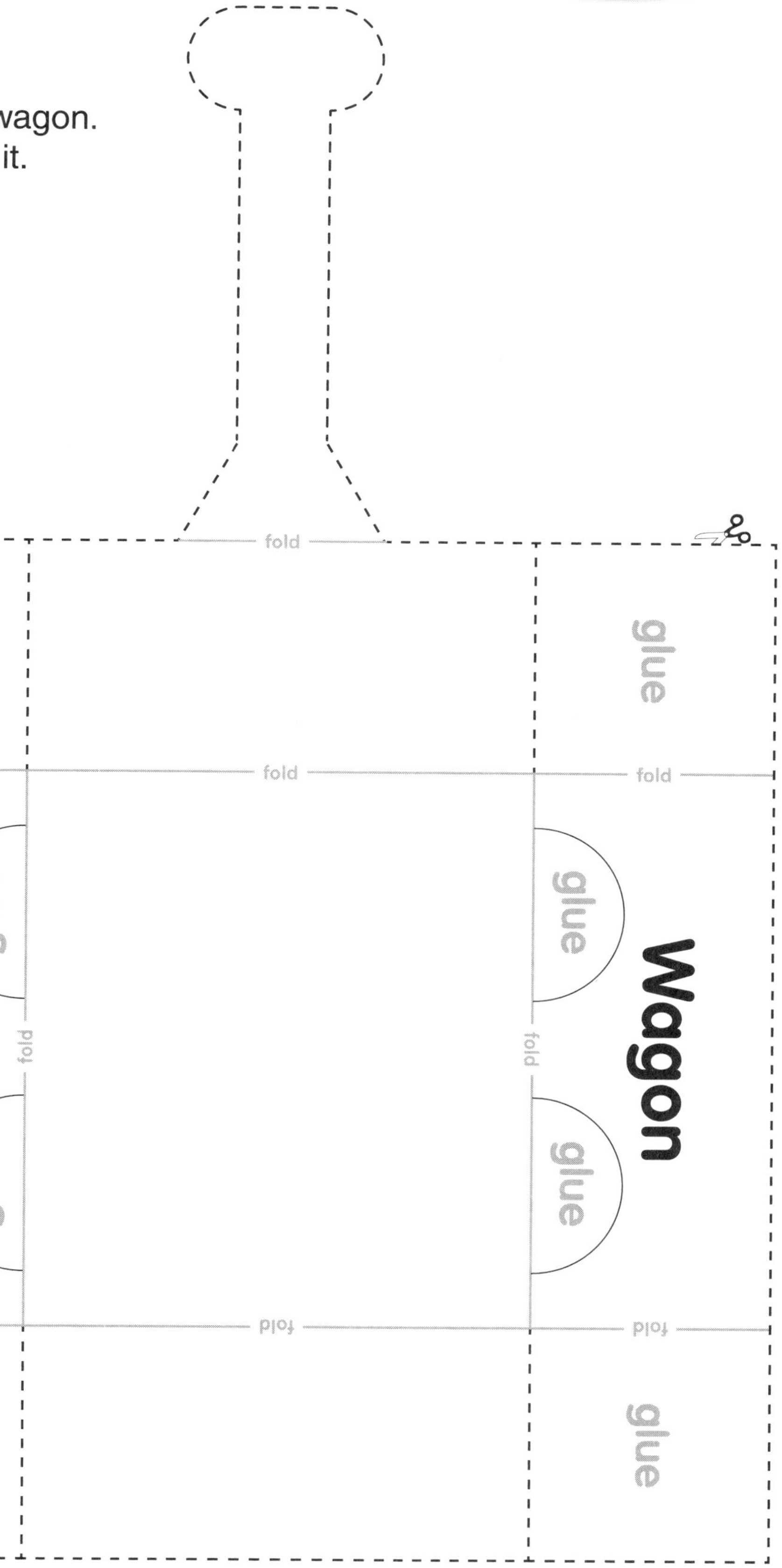

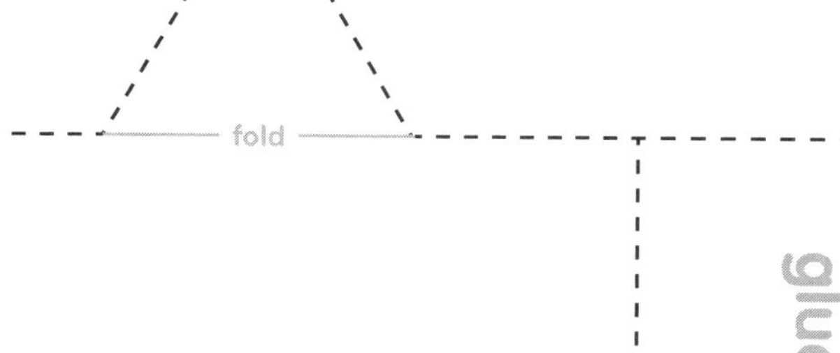

fold

glue

glue

fold

fold

fold

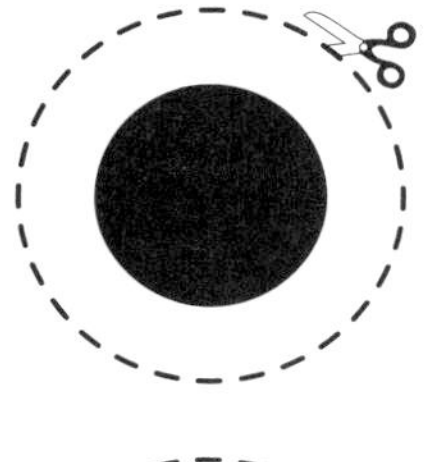

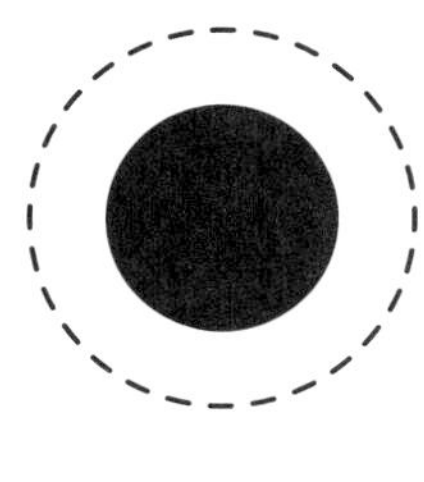

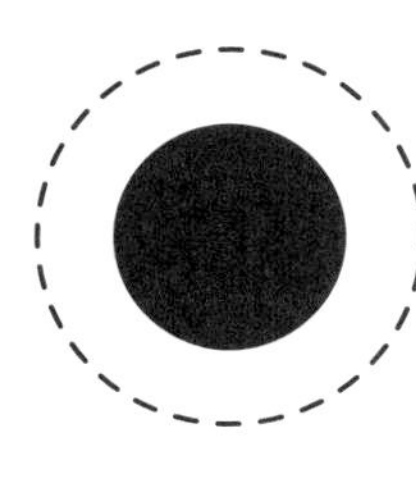

glue

glue

Wagon

fold

glue

glue

Wagon

fold

glue

glue

fold

fold

fold

glue

glue

Skills: Follow multi-step directions; practice oral language and small motor skills.

Picture Dictionary

horses

ladder

hose

blocks

toys

Trucks

Name

See the trucks, big and small.
Watch them work. They do it all.

Farm trucks carry hay and horses.

2

Big rig trucks carry gas and food.

Firetrucks carry ladders and hoses.

3

My trucks carry blocks and toys.

See the trucks, big and small. Watch them work. They do it all.

Name ____________________

What Did the Story Say?

Write the words on the lines to tell what the story said.

blocks	hay	gas	hoses
ladders	food	toys	horses

Farm trucks carry

__________ and __________.

Big rig trucks carry

__________ and __________.

Firetrucks carry

__________ and __________.

Toy trucks carry

__________ and __________.

 Skill: Recall story details.

Name ______________________________

Opposites

Color, cut, and glue to show things that are **heavy** and things that are **light**.

heavy

glue	glue
glue	glue

light

glue	glue
glue	glue

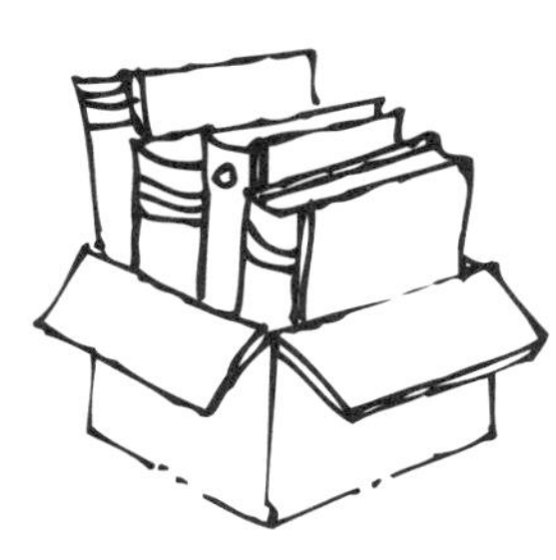

Skills: Identify opposites; classify objects into categories; follow multi-step directions.

Name ______________________________

Add –er

Write each word to name a person.

1. farm + er = ___ ___ ___ ___ ___ ___

2. build + er = ___ ___ ___ ___ ___ ___ ___

3. paint + er = ___ ___ ___ ___ ___ ___ ___

4. teach + er = ___ ___ ___ ___ ___ ___ ___

5. jump + er = ___ ___ ___ ___ ___ ___

6. play + er = ___ ___ ___ ___ ___ ___

Write the number in the circle to show what each person would use.

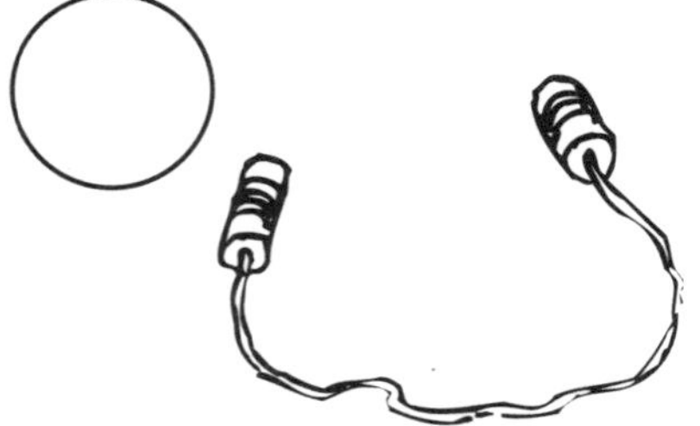

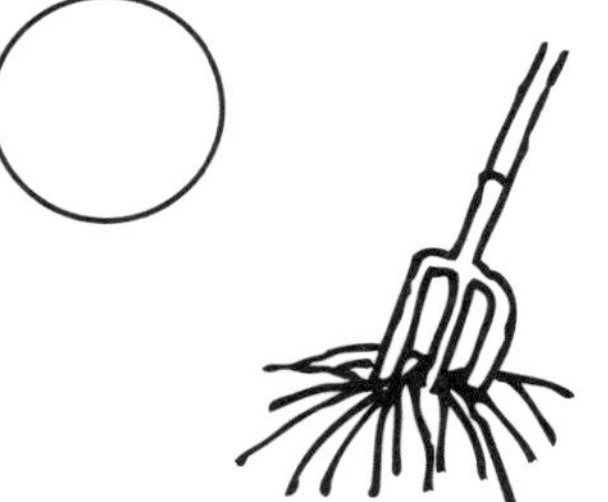

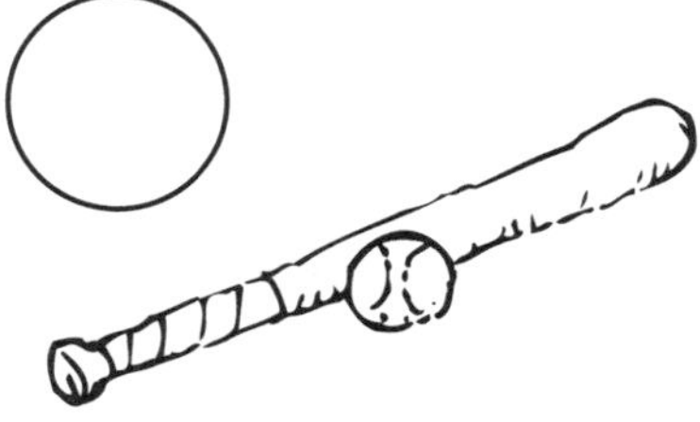

 Skills: Add a suffix to change word meaning; make inferences; develop vocabulary.

Name ______________________

Find the Mystery Word

Do the puzzle to find the mystery word.

1. 

2. 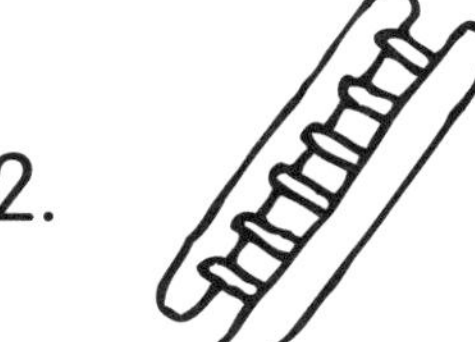

3. 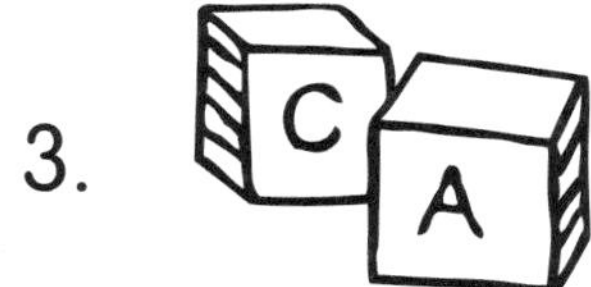

4. 

The mystery word is ___ ___ u ___ k ___.

campfire

snap hoo whoosh

sounds

owl

sleeping bag

The Campfire

____
Name

1

The night is dark. I hear sounds. They are keeping me awake.

2

The wind whispers. An owl hoots. Did I see something move?

3

I am safe in my sleeping bag. The campfire is warm and bright. I'm glad I have the campfire. Good night.

Name ______________________

What Did the Story Say?

Write a sentence to answer each question.

Where is the boy?

____

____

What is the boy doing?

____

____

Why is the boy glad he has the campfire?

____

____

 Skills: Recall story details; answer questions with complete sentences.

Name ________________________________

Camping

Look at the picture. Use the words in the box to complete the sentences.

over the campfire	ready	a tent
in his sleeping bag	in the forest	

The boy is camping ________________________________.

He has already put up ________________________________.

The cooking pot is ________________________________.

Soon, dinner will be ________________________________.

The boy will sleep ________________________________.

Camping is fun!

Skills: Use context and picture clues to complete sentences; practice critical thinking.

Name ______________________________

"Fire" Words

Write the two words that make each compound word.

campfire ____________ + ____________

firefly ____________ + ____________

fireplace ____________ + ____________

firewood ____________ + ____________

fireworks ____________ + ____________

firefighter ____________ + ____________

firecracker ____________ + ____________

backfire ____________ + ____________

firetruck ____________ + ____________

fireproof ____________ + ____________

Skill: Divide compound words into their original word forms.

Name ____________________

Action Words

Use the words in the box to fill in the blanks.

keep	move	hear
sleep	whispers	hoots

I ___ ___ ___ ___ sounds.

They ___ ___ ___ ___ me awake.

The wind ___ ___ ___ ___ ___ ___ ___ ___.

An owl ___ ___ ___ ___ ___.

Did something ___ ___ ___ ___?

I will ___ ___ ___ ___ ___ by the campfire.

Circle the words that rhyme in each row.

hear	afraid	fire	fear
bag	see	flee	dark
owl	toot	sound	hoot

Skills: Use context clues to complete sentences; recognize and use action words; identify rhyming words.

Picture Dictionary

pulled

raked

planted

watered

Ally's Garden

____

Name

1

Ally wanted a garden. She pulled the weeds. She raked the dirt. She planted the seeds.

2

Ally watered her garden. Little plants grew in the sun. Ally watered the plants. They grew bigger and bigger.

3

Soon, the plants had surprises. Ally got a big basket. She picked good things to eat. Ally likes having a garden.

Name ______________________________

What Did the Story Say?

Answer each question to tell what the story said.
Fill in the circle next to the correct answer.

What did Ally do first to get her garden ready?

- ○ plant the seeds
- ○ water the plants
- ○ pull the weeds

What did Ally do to help her garden grow?

- ○ watch the plants
- ○ water the plants
- ○ pick the plants

What did Ally get from her garden?

- ○ good things to eat
- ○ a big basket
- ○ seeds

Did Ally like having a garden? ○ yes ○ no

Will Ally plant a garden next year? ○ yes ○ no

Draw and label three things you would plant in a garden.

______________ ______________ ______________

 Skills: Recall story details; practice critical thinking.

Name ______________________________

Rhyme Time

Match the words that rhyme.

weeds •	• ants
rake •	• seeds
plants •	• heat
grew •	• trick
pick •	• make
eat •	• new

Use the words to complete each sentence. Write the word that rhymes with the word in **bold** letters.

Red **ants** crawled on the ______________________.

Pull the **weeds** before you plant the ______________________.

The **new** plants ______________________ quickly.

You have to **rake** the dirt to ______________________ a garden.

Skills: Identify rhyming words; use context clues to complete sentences.

Name ______________________________

Making a Garden

Write sentences to tell how to make a garden.

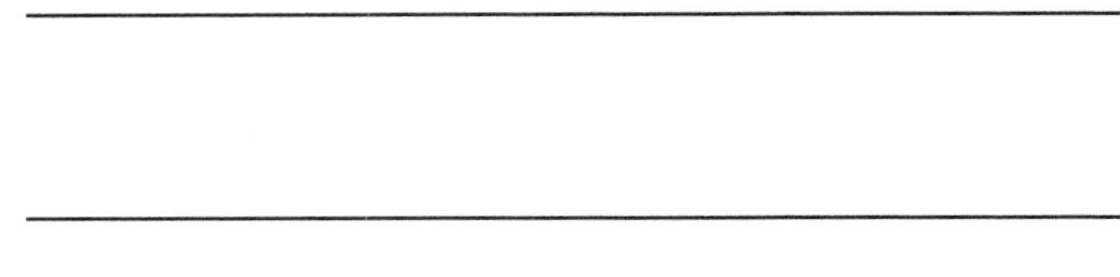

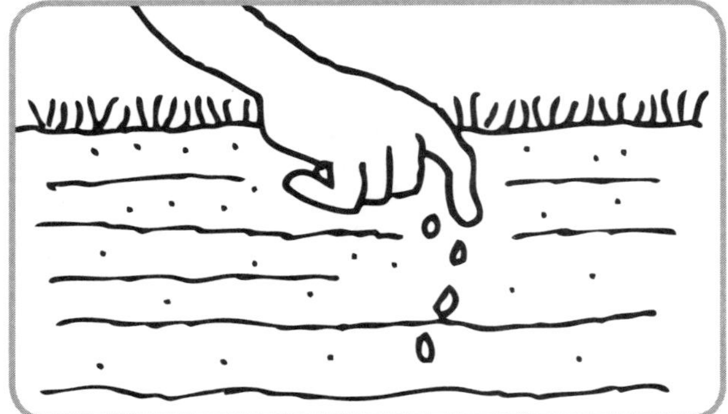

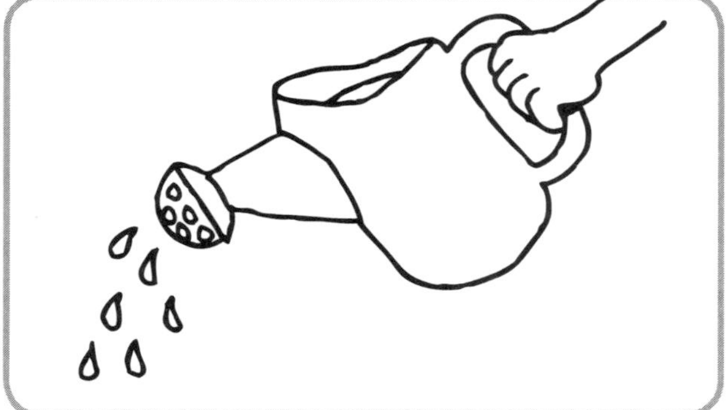

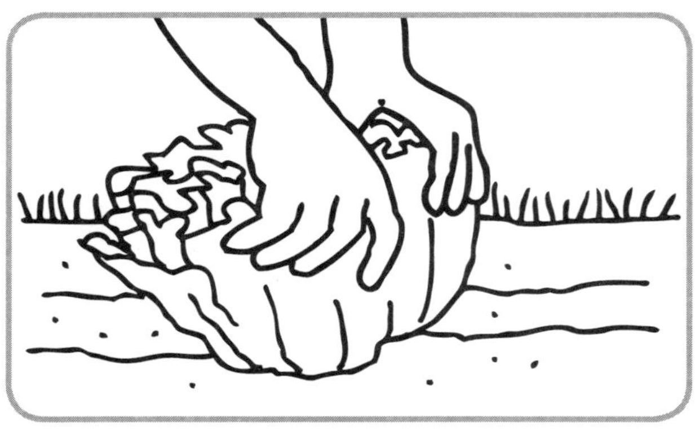

 Skills: Use picture clues to write about a sequence of events; write complete sentences.

Name ____________________

Tools for the Garden

Match the tools to the jobs. Write the names of the tools on the lines. Use the words in the box to help you.

shovel	watering can	hoe	rake

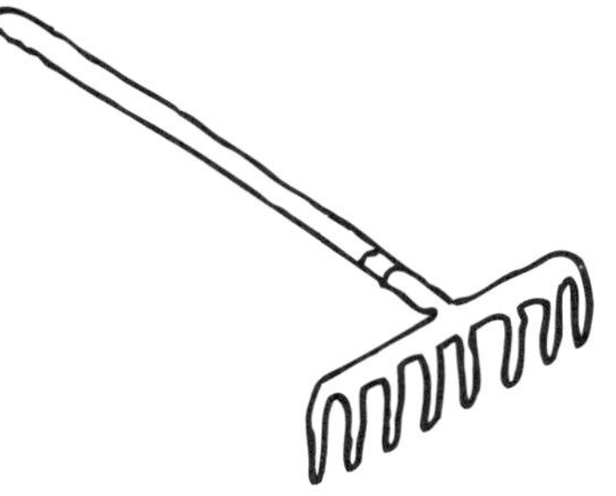

- makes rows for planting

____

- feeds the little plants

____

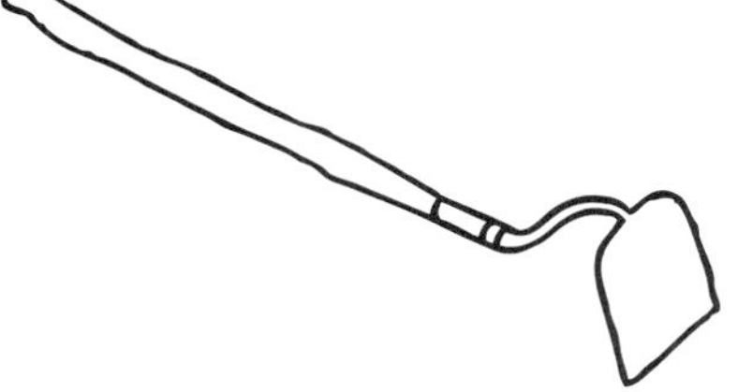

- smooths out the soil

____

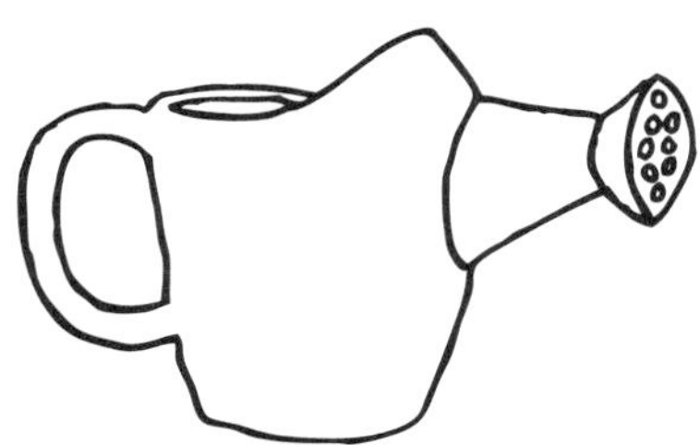

- digs holes in the dirt

____

Picture Dictionary

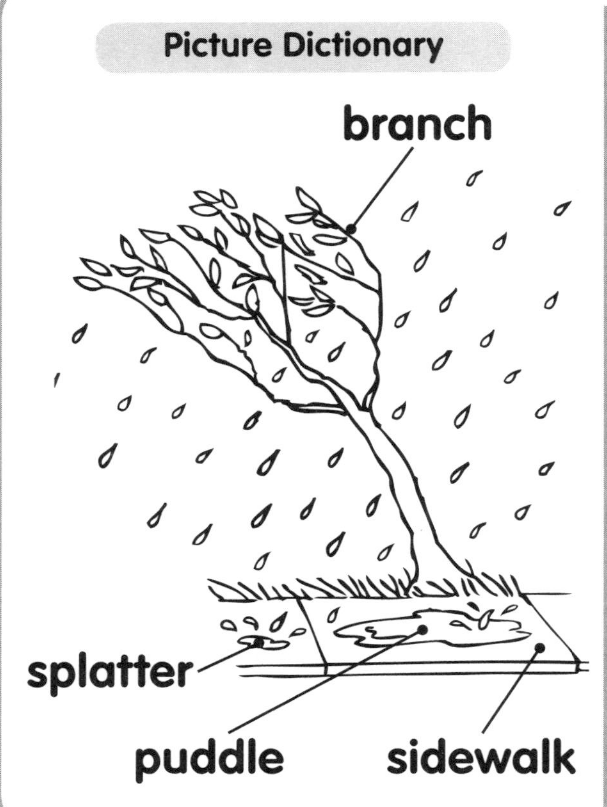

Rainy Day Fun

Name

1

Rain is splattering on the sidewalk. The wind is blowing branches against the window. What can we do on such a rainy day?

We can't play on the slide at the park. We can't fly a kite on the hill. We can't ride a bike around the block. What can we do?

We can jump in puddles. We can hide under my umbrella. We can have lots of fun on a rainy day. Splish! Splash! Splosh!

Name ______________________________

What Did the Story Say?

Write sentences to answer the questions.

What kind of a day is it?

____

What is splattering on the sidewalk?

____

____

Why can't the boy and his dog play at the park?

____

____

What can the boy and his dog do?

____

____

What would you do on a rainy day?

____

____

 Skills: Recall story details; answer questions with complete sentences; relate personal experience to text; practice critical thinking.

Name ___________________________

Working with Word Families

The **–ide** word family can help you learn new words. Write the words.

h + ide = ____ ____ ____ ____

s + ide = ____ ____ ____ ____

r + ide = ____ ____ ____ ____

t + ide = ____ ____ ____ ____

w + ide = ____ ____ ____ ____

sl + ide = ____ ____ ____ ____ ____

br + ide = ____ ____ ____ ____ ____

Use the words to complete the sentences.

The boy will ______________ under his umbrella.

I want to ______________ down the hill on my sled.

My mom showed me how to ______________ a horse.

The ______________ wore a beautiful white dress.

Skills: Read common word families **–ide**; use context clues to complete sentences.

Name ____________________

Splash, Splosh, Splatter

Write **splash** on the line. Then draw what will make the splash.

The rock will ____________________ in the lake.

Write **splosh** on the line. Then draw what you can splosh with.

I can ____________________ in the puddle with my boots on.

Write **splatter** on the line. Then draw what will splatter.

The rain will ____________________ on the window.

 Skill: Develop vocabulary related to a theme.

Name ________________________________

Rainy Day Fun

Make a list of five things that you might like to do on a rainy day.

1. ____

2. ____

3. ____

4. ____

5. ____

Draw a picture of yourself doing one of the things on your list.

Skills: Relate personal experience to text; practice critical thinking.

Picture Dictionary

North Pole

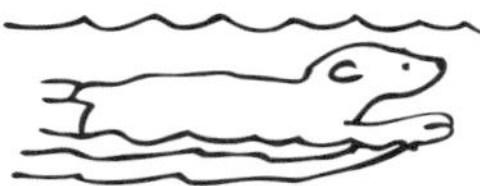

swim

paddle

shake

The Polar Bear

Name

1

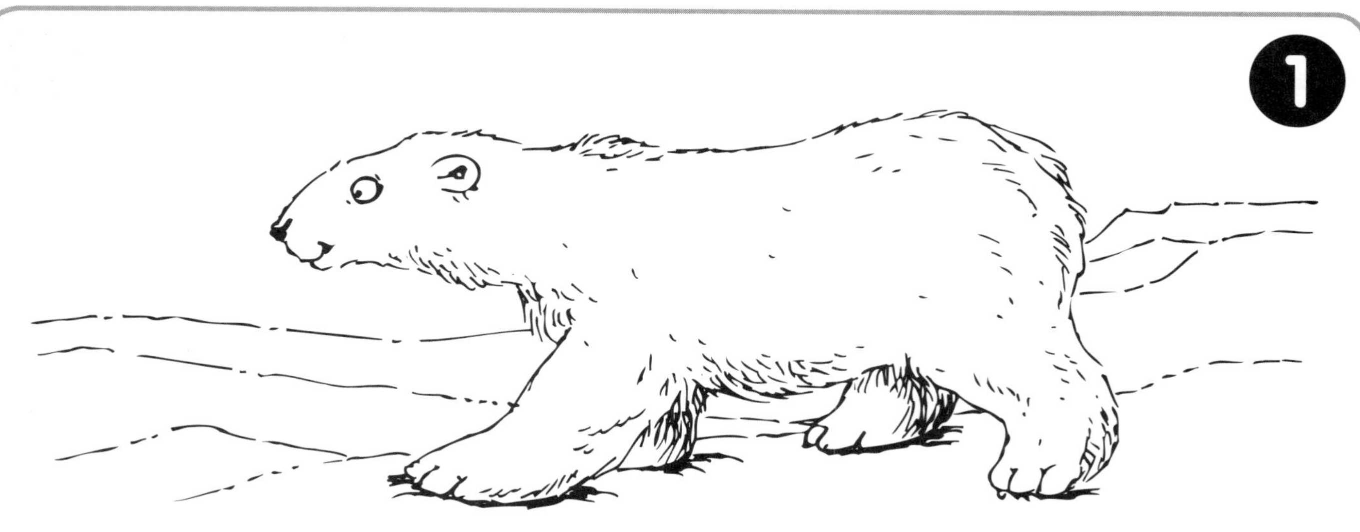

The polar bear lives near the North Pole. It walks on snow and ice. It has fur on the bottom of its feet. The fur keeps the bear's feet warm.

The polar bear swims in icy water. It is a good swimmer. It paddles with its front legs. It pulls its back legs along behind.

The polar bear dries off after it swims. It shakes the water off its fur. Shake, shake, shake. The North Pole is a very cold place. Brrr!

Name ______________________

What Did the Story Say?

Write sentences to tell what the story said.

I learned three things about polar bears:

1. ______________________
____

2. ______________________
____

3. ______________________
____

Would a polar bear live in the desert? yes no

Tell why or why not.

____
____
____
____

 Skills: Organize information after reading; write complete sentences; relate prior knowledge to story text; practice critical thinking.

Name ______________________________

Working with Word Families

The **–ear** word family can help you learn new words. Write the words.

b + ear = ___ ___ ___ ___

t + ear = ___ ___ ___ ___

w + ear = ___ ___ ___ ___

p + ear = ___ ___ ___ ___

Use the words to complete the sentences.

I need to ______________ a warm coat today.

The polar ______________ likes cold places.

Did you eat a ______________?

My shirt had a ______________ in it.

Write your own sentence using an **–ear** word.

____

____

Skills: Read common word families **–ear**; use context clues to complete sentences.

Name ______________________________

Add *–ing*

To add **–ing** to some words, you have to double the final consonant.

swi**m** + ing = swi**mm**ing

Double the final consonant and add **–ing**.

run + ing = ___ ___ ___ ___ ___ ___ ___

tap + ing = ___ ___ ___ ___ ___ ___ ___

stop + ing = ___ ___ ___ ___ ___ ___ ___ ___

hit + ing = ___ ___ ___ ___ ___ ___ ___

flip + ing = ___ ___ ___ ___ ___ ___ ___ ___

Write a sentence using one of the **–ing** words.

____

____

Mark which rule you learned from these words.

____ Double the final consonant in some words when you add **–ing**.

____ Add **s** to a word to mean **more than one**.

Name ____________________

A Polar Bear Puzzle

Read the clues and fill in the squares. Use the words in the box to help you.

bears
warm
feet
fur
swim

Across

1. A polar bear has ____ on its body.
2. Polar ____ are good swimmers.
4. Fur helps the polar bear stay ____.

Down

1. A polar bear has four ____.
3. Polar bears can ____ in icy water.

Skills: Recall story details; use context clues to complete sentences; follow multi-step directions.

Picture Dictionary

move

push

sail

latch

Moving Air

Name

1

The wind is moving air.
It can be very strong.
It can lift and push a hat
And move that hat along.

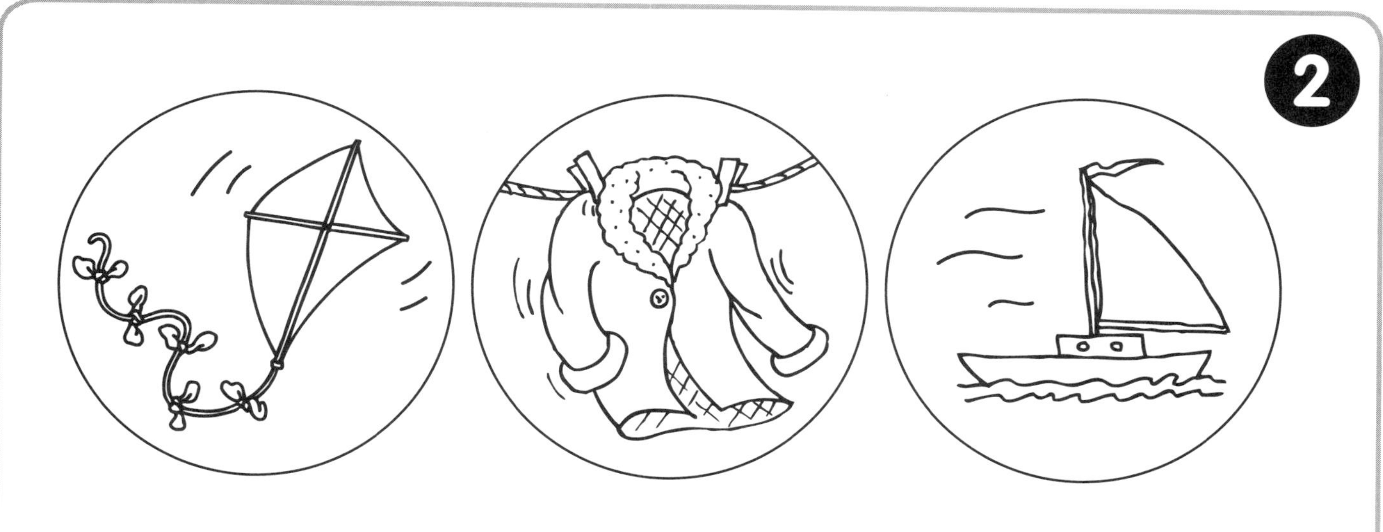

The wind is moving air.
It can fly a kite.
It dries a coat and sails a boat.
The wind moves day and night.

The wind is moving air,
And moving air is great,
Unless I forget to close the latch,
And it opens up the gate!

Name ______________________

What Did the Story Say?

Circle **yes** or **no** to tell what the story said.

The wind can wear a hat.	yes	no
The wind can make a kite fly.	yes	no
The wind can move a boat.	yes	no
The wind can drink water.	yes	no
The wind can open a latch.	yes	no
The wind can be strong.	yes	no

What do you think the wind can and cannot do?
Complete each sentence below.

The wind can ______________________________

______________________________.

The wind cannot ______________________________

______________________________.

 Skills: Recall story details; practice critical thinking; relate prior knowledge to story text; answer *yes* or *no* questions.

Name ______________________________

Working with Word Families

The **–atch** word family can help you learn new words. Write the words.

l + atch = ___ ___ ___ ___ ___

b + atch = ___ ___ ___ ___ ___

c + atch = ___ ___ ___ ___ ___

h + atch = ___ ___ ___ ___ ___

m + atch = ___ ___ ___ ___ ___

p + atch = ___ ___ ___ ___ ___

scr + atch = ___ ___ ___ ___ ___ ___ ___

Use the words to complete the sentences.

Mom needs to sew a ______________ on my pants.

I can ______________ the football.

Dad made a ______________ of cookies.

One red sock and one blue sock do not ______________.

Skills: Read common word families **–atch**; use context clues to complete sentences.

Name ________________________________

Action Words

Circle the action word in each sentence.

The dog ran through the open gate.

My kite flies above the trees.

A boat sailed on the water.

The farmer drives a tractor.

The wind blows the leaves around.

Write an action word to complete each sentence.

The students ____________________ lunch.

The girls ____________________ a game.

The kitten ____________________ on my bed.

He ____________________ the ball over the fence.

The bird ____________________ to its nest.

 Skill: Identify and use action words.

Name ______________________

Crossword Puzzle

Read the clues and fill in the squares. Use the words in the box to help you.

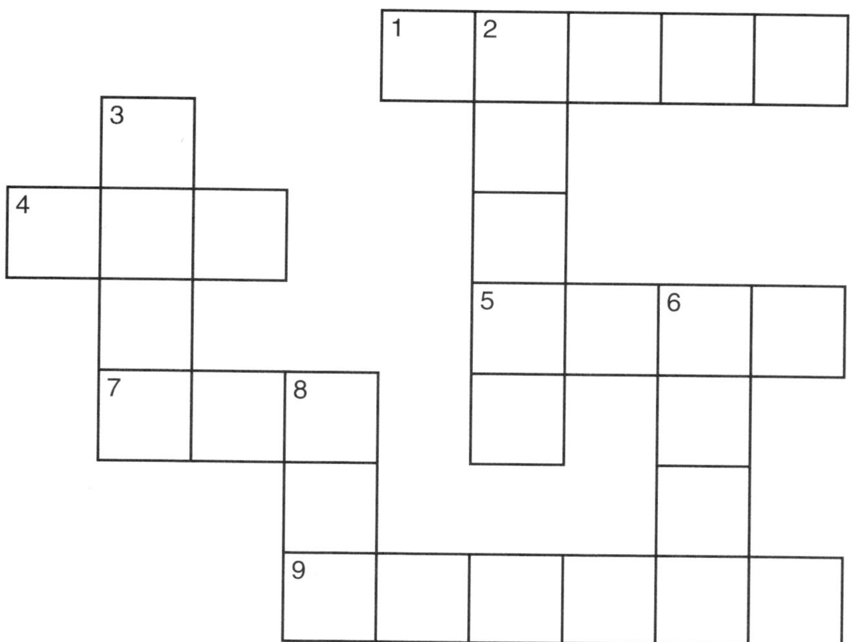

dry
wind
yes
air
strong
cool
flies
open
latch

Across

1. A kite _____ in the air.
4. Wind is moving _____.
5. I feel the _____ wind blow.
7. The wind can _____ a coat.
9. The wind can be very _____.

Down

2. Close the _____ on the gate.
3. The _____ blows the leaves along.
6. The wind can _____ a gate.
8. Can you hear the wind blow?

Skills: Use context clues to complete sentences; follow multi-step directions.

Picture Dictionary

mouse

bunny

fox

ladybug

Sam's Blue Hat

Name

1

Sam had a blue hat. It had a little bell on it. Sam lost his hat in the woods one day.

A little mouse saw Sam's hat. It looked soft and warm, so the mouse moved right in.

Then a bunny saw Sam's hat, and the bunny hopped right in.

2

Then a fox saw Sam's hat, and he snuggled in.

Then a ladybug saw Sam's hat, and she crawled in.

3

KABOOM!

That was too much! Sam's blue hat ripped to pieces.

The mouse was sad.
The bunny was sad.
The fox was sad.
The ladybug was sad.

All that was left was the little bell.

Name ______________________________

What Did the Story Say?

Write sentences to answer the questions.

What happened to Sam's hat?

____

____

____

What was left at the end of the story?

____

____

Color the hat and draw the first animal that moved in.

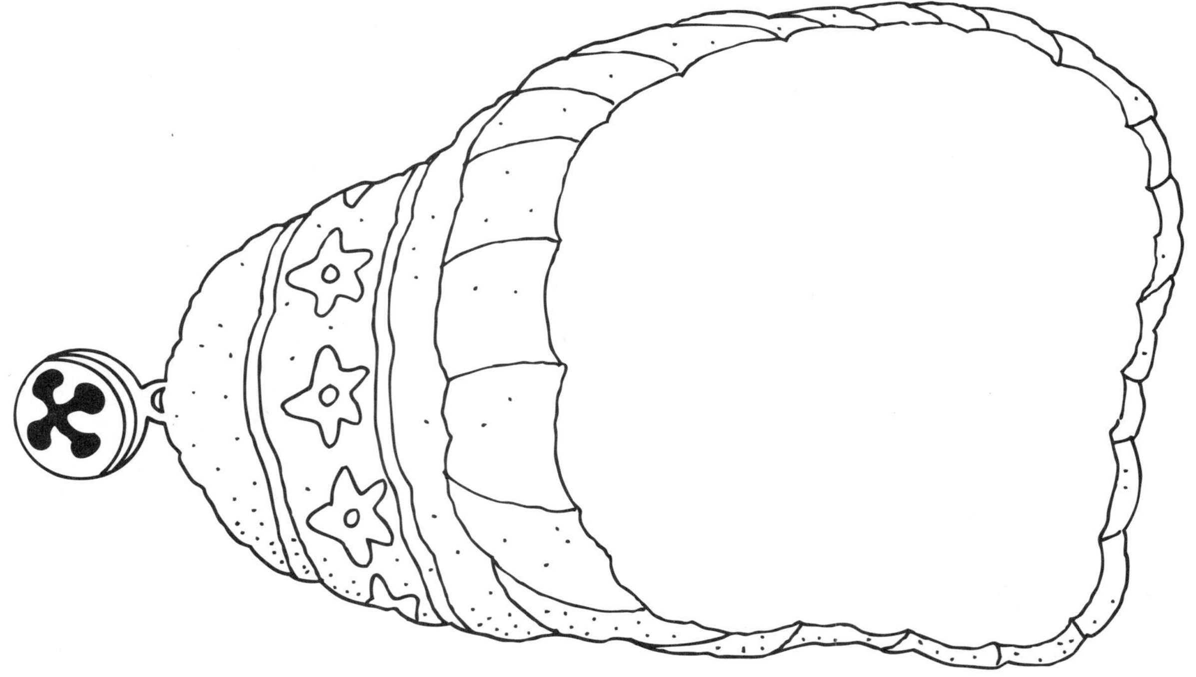

 Skills: Recall story details; answer questions with complete sentences.

Name ______________________________

Put Them in Order

Cut and glue to show the order in the story.

Who saw Sam's hat?

first	glue	second	glue
third	glue	fourth	glue

KABOOM!

All that was left was the little bell.

Name ______________________

Who Does It Belong To?

Adding **'s** to a word shows that something belongs to a person or thing.
Circle each word with **'s**. Write the word on the line that tells who it belongs to.

The bunny's ears are big.

The ears belong to the ______________________.

The bunny sat on the mouse's tail.

The tail belongs to the ______________________.

The ladybug's spots are black.

The spots belong to the ______________________.

The fox's nose is long and pointed.

The nose belongs to the ______________________.

Sam's hat had a little bell on it.

The hat belongs to ______________________.

 Skill: Identify possessive nouns.

Name ______________________________

Big, Bigger, Biggest

Write the correct word from the box to label each picture.

____

____

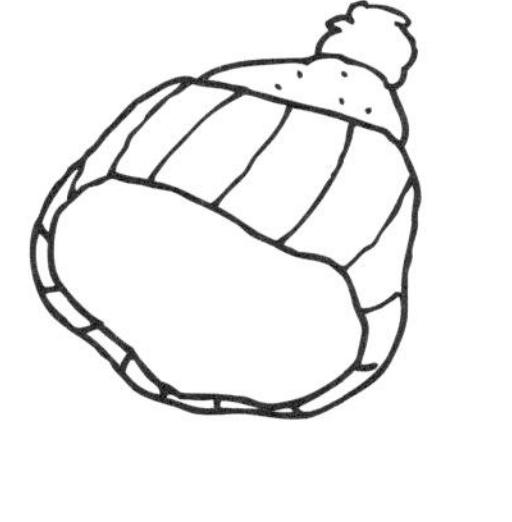

____

big	bigger	biggest

Use the words in the box to complete the sentences.

Sam's hat was ______________________ than the mouse.

The fox was the ______________________ animal in Sam's hat.

The bunny has ______________________ ears.

Is the bell ______________________ than the ladybug?

The ______________________ animals of all are in the zoo.

Skill: Use comparative and superlative adjectives.

Picture Dictionary

nibble

kibble

snuggle

Sparky

Name

1

Sparky is my puppy.
He loves to jump and run.
When I come home from school each day,
He's ready to have fun.

2

Sparky is my puppy.
He loves to lick and nibble.
I put his dish down on the rug,
And he eats all his kibble.

3

Sparky is my puppy.
He loves to take a nap.
I pet my puppy softly
As he snuggles on my lap.

Name ________________________________

What Did the Story Say?

Use the words in the box to complete each sentence.

a rug	a nap	kibble	a puppy

Sparky is ________________________.

I put his dish on ________________________.

He eats ________________________.

He loves to take ________________________.

Add **'s** to Sparky's name to show things that belong to him.

Sparky____ dish

Sparky____ rug

Sparky____ kibble

Sparky____ nose

 Skills: Recall story details; add **'s** to make possessive nouns.

Name ______________________________

Words That Tell *Where*

Use a phrase from the box to complete each sentence below.

in the yard	on the rug
at the pet store	on my lap

I got Sparky ______________________________.

I play with Sparky ______________________________.

Sparky's dish of kibble is ______________________________.

Sparky snuggles ______________________________.

Name ____________________

Rhyme Time

Fill in the circle next to the ending that makes a rhyme.

My puppy loves to nibble

- ○ on a plate of ham.
- ○ on a dish of kibble.
- ○ on a box of cookies.

My puppy likes to chase a stick

- ○ and then hide it.
- ○ and then bring it to me.
- ○ and then give me a lick.

My puppy sits on my lap

- ○ and licks my face.
- ○ and takes a nap.
- ○ and barks at the cat.

Write rhyming words on the lines.

dish	rug	lap
________	________	________
________	________	________
________	________	________

 Skill: Read and write rhyming words.

Name ______________________________

Compound Words

Circle the compound words in this rhyme.

Inside, outside, upside down.
Sparky acts just like a clown.

Circle **yes** or **no** to tell which words are compound words.

cannot	yes	no
puppy	yes	no
running	yes	no
birthday	yes	no
funny	yes	no
something	yes	no
bathtub	yes	no
jumping	yes	no

Skill: Identify compound words.

Picture Dictionary

see

hear

touch

smell

taste

It's Morning

____

Name

Wake up! It's morning.
What do you see?
I see the sun,
And it's shining on me.

Wake up! It's morning.
What do you hear?
A robin is singing
A song loud and clear.

2

Wake up! It's morning.
What do you touch?
I touch the soft blanket
That I like so much.

Wake up! It's morning.
What do you smell?
Someone is baking
Fresh bread. I can tell.

3

Wake up! It's morning.
What do you eat?
I eat warm oats with honey
To make them taste sweet.

Wake up! It's morning.
What do you do?
I jump out of bed
And get ready for school.

Name ___________________________

Using My Senses

Complete the sentences to tell what you **see**, **hear**, **touch**, **smell**, and **taste** in the morning.

I **see** ____________________________________

____.

I **hear** ____________________________________

____.

I **touch** ___________________________________

____.

I **smell** ___________________________________

____.

I **taste** ___________________________________

____.

 Skills: Relate personal experience to text; write complete sentences.

Name ______________________________

I or *Me*?

Use **I** when you are the person doing something.

I bake cookies with my mom.

Use **me** when something happens to you.

Mom gave **me** a cookie.

Fill in each blank with **I** or **me**.

__________ have fun cooking.

Dad and __________ make cookies.

He lets __________ help.

__________ put in flour and sugar.

Dad helps __________ mix the batter.

__________ put the cookies on a plate.

Dad lets __________ taste one.

__________ think our cookies taste good.

Name ______________________________

Action Words

Color the action words.

sun

song

bread

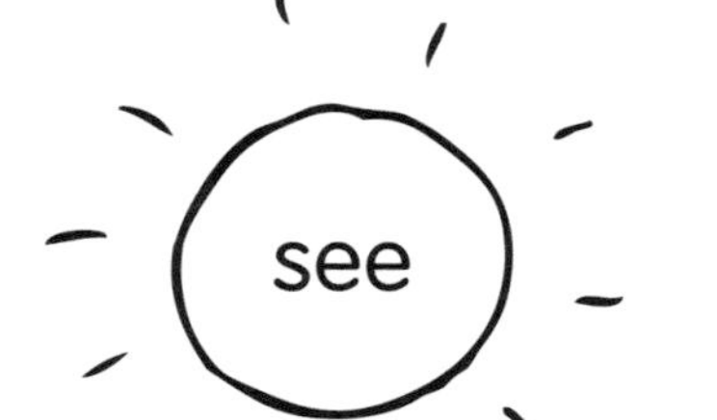

hear

Use the words in the box to fill in the missing action words.

hear	smell	ran

I ____________________ an egg frying.

We ____________________ a bell ringing.

The dog ____________________ across the street.

 Skill: Identify and use action words.

Name ________________________________

Rhyme Time

Read each word. Add the ending letters to make words that rhyme.

wag	fl________	dr________
row	sh________	sn________
top	dr________	sh________
sick	ch________	tr________
hide	br________	sl________
tap	tr________	cl________
town	cl________	br________
bin	sk________	ch________
cake	sn________	fl________
date	sl________	sk________

Skill: Use initial consonant blends to create rhyming words.

Picture Dictionary

squirrel

turtle

insect

Hide-and-Seek

Name

1

Do you like to play hide-and-seek? It is a fun game. Some animals play hide-and-seek, too. Hiding is more than a game for these animals. Hiding helps keep the animals safe.

2

Some animals hide in their houses. A squirrel hides in its hole. A turtle hides inside its shell. Hiding helps keep the animals safe.

3

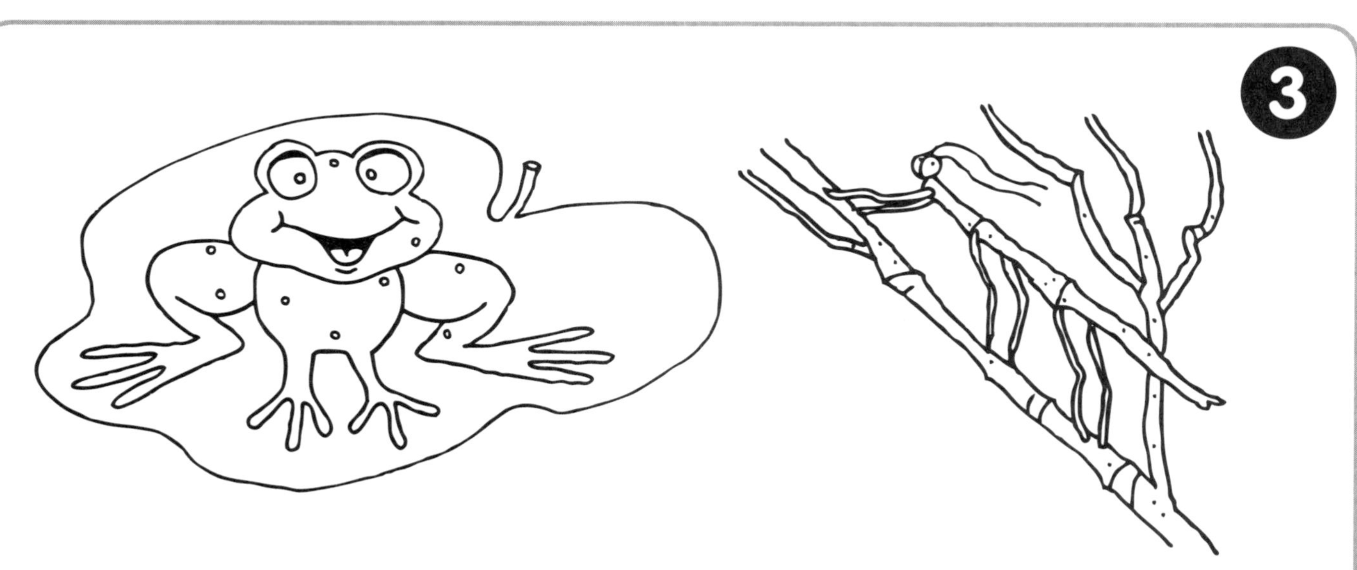

Some animals look like the places they hide in. A green frog sits on a green leaf. A brown insect sits on a brown stick. Hiding helps keep the animals safe.

Name ______________________

What Did the Story Say?

Draw lines to show where each animal hides.

squirrel •	• inside its shell
frog •	• on a stick
turtle •	• in its hole
insect •	• on a leaf

Write a sentence to tell why animals hide.

____

____

Circle **yes** or **no**.

I like to play hide-and-seek.	yes	no
I hide to keep safe.	yes	no
Some animals hide to keep safe.	yes	no

 Skills: Recall story details; write a complete sentence; relate personal experience to text; answer *yes* or *no* questions.

Name ________________________________

Listen for the Vowel

Say the names of the pictures in each box.
Circle the vowel you hear in all the names.

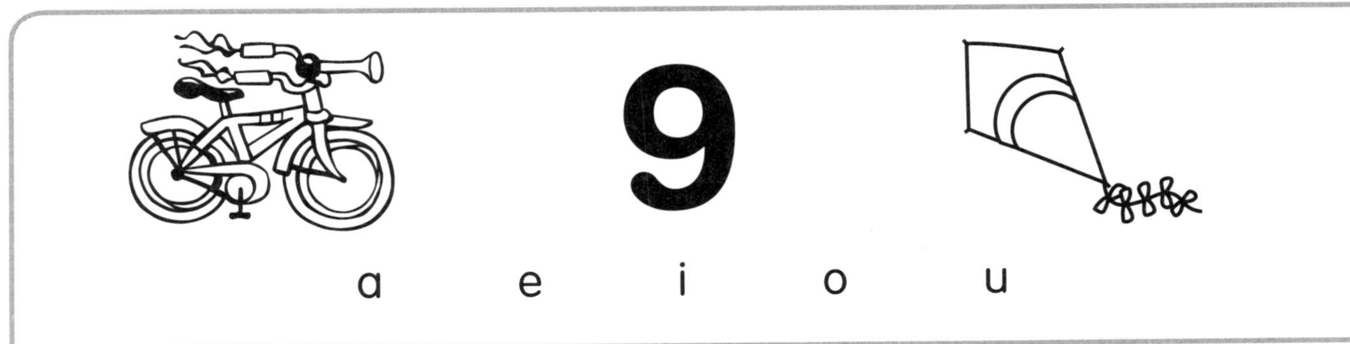

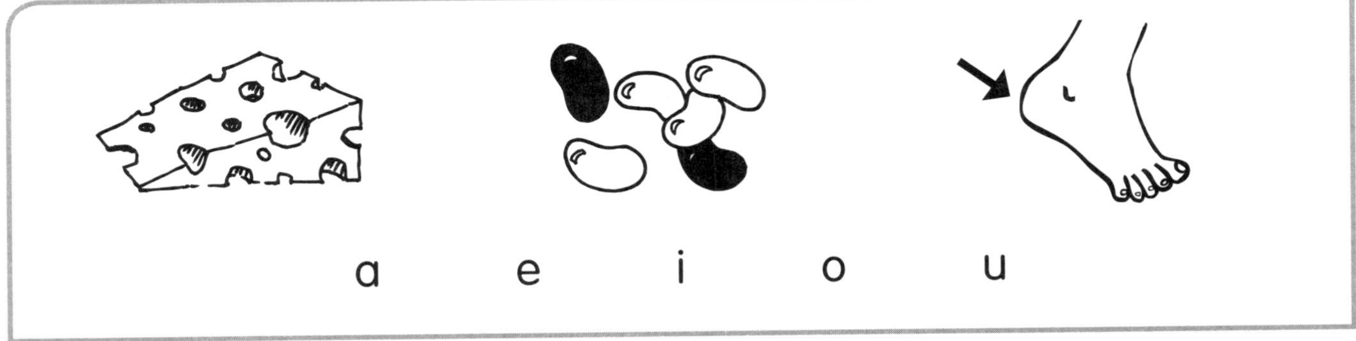

Skill: Identify long and short vowel sounds.

Name ______________________________

Find the Mystery Word

Do the crossword puzzle to find the mystery word.

Down

1. It hides in a hole.
3. It hides on a leaf.
4. It hides on a stick.

Across

2. Animals hide to keep _____.
5. Children play hide-and-_____.
6. It hides inside its shell.

The mystery word is h __ d __ n __.

 Skills: Recall information from text; develop vocabulary related to a theme; practice spelling.

Name ___________________________________

Hide the Animals

Some animals use color to help them hide.
An animal changes its color to match a hiding place.

Color to help the animals hide. Then write to tell where they are hiding.

A frog hides on ______________________.

A stick insect hides on ______________________.

Skills: Use picture clues to complete sentences; follow multi-step directions.

Zack's Sandwich

Name

This is Zack.

This is the slice of **bread**
that started the sandwich
that Zack made.

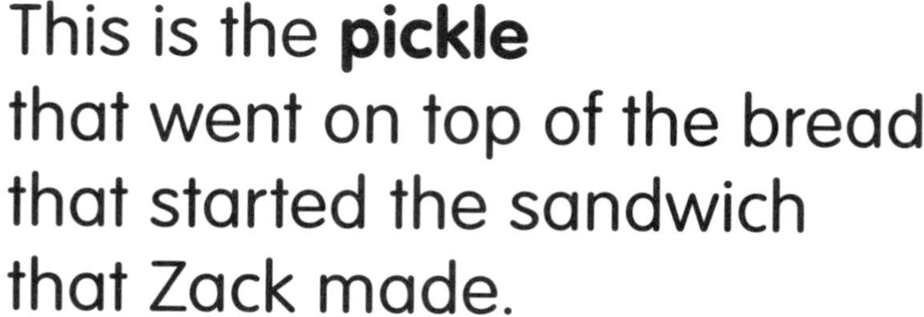

This is the **pickle**
that went on top of the bread
that started the sandwich
that Zack made.

2

This is the **ham**
that covered the pickle
that went on top of the bread
that started the sandwich
that Zack made.

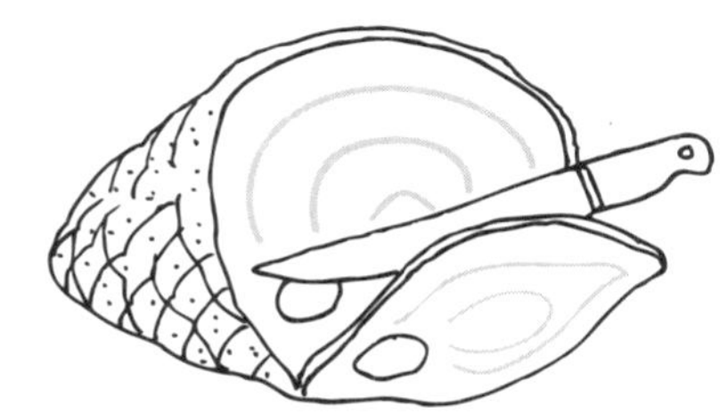

This is the **lettuce**
that sat on the ham
that covered the pickle
that went on top of the bread
that started the sandwich
that Zack made.

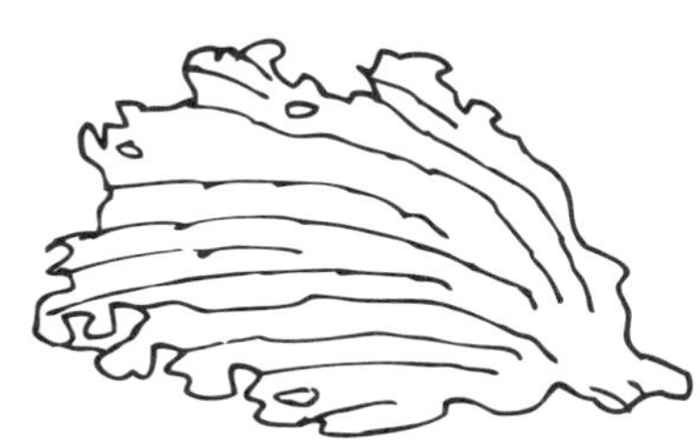

3

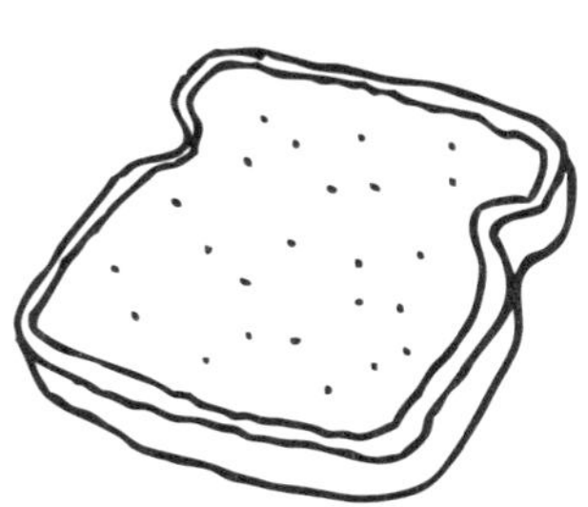

This is the slice of bread
that came after the lettuce
that sat on the ham
that covered the pickle
that went on top of the bread
that started the sandwich
that Zack made.

This is the **sandwich**
that Zack made!

Name ____________________

What Did the Story Say?

Write a recipe for making Zack's sandwich.
Then draw a picture to show how the sandwich will look.

Zack's Sandwich

Recipe

Ingredients:

____

____

____

____

What to do:

1. ____________________
2. ____________________
3. ____________________
4. ____________________
5. ____________________

 Skills: Recall story details; organize information after reading.

Name ____________________

Working with Word Families

The **–ice** word family can help you learn new words. Write the words.

sl + ice = ___ ___ ___ ___ ___

d + ice = ___ ___ ___ ___

m + ice = ___ ___ ___ ___

pr + ice = ___ ___ ___ ___ ___

tw + ice = ___ ___ ___ ___ ___

sp + ice = ___ ___ ___ ___ ___

Use the words to complete the sentences.

The ____________ ran into their hole.

Can you tell me the ____________ of that hat?

Roll the ____________ to play the game.

May I have a ____________ of apple pie?

Skills: Read common word families **–ice**; use context clues to complete sentences.

Name ___________________________

Compare and Contrast

Read this Mother Goose rhyme called "This Is the House That Jack Built." Tell how it is like "Zack's Sandwich." Tell how it is different.

This is the house that Jack built.

This is the malt
That lay in the house that Jack built.

This is the rat,
That ate the malt
That lay in the house that Jack built.

This is the cat,
That killed the rat,
That ate the malt
That lay in the house that Jack built.

This is the dog,
That worried the cat,
That killed the rat,
That ate the malt
That lay in the house that Jack built.

This is the cow with the crumpled horn,
That tossed the dog,
That worried the cat,
That killed the rat,
That ate the malt
That lay in the house that Jack built.

 Skills: Compare and contrast similar stories; practice critical thinking.

Name ______________________________

Think About It

Write a sentence to answer each question.

Does a sandwich always have two slices of bread?

____

____

Is a hot dog a sandwich?

____

____

What is the funniest sandwich you ever ate?

____

____

What name would you give Zack's sandwich?

____

____

Skills: Answer questions with complete sentences; practice critical thinking.

Circle the double letters in each word.

tomorrow

bunny

carrots

kitten

fuzzy

puppy

happy

The Pet Show

Name

1

We are having a pet show at school tomorrow.
Nick will bring his bunny named Wiggles.
It is black and white. It likes to nibble carrots.

2

Sara will bring her orange and white kitten. She calls it Fluffy because it is soft and fuzzy. Fluffy likes to jump and play. Fluffy wears a bell so Sara can always tell where her kitten is.

3

I will bring my puppy to the pet show. His name is Skipper. I am teaching him to sit. Skipper is happy when he gets a treat. He wags his tail and licks my face.

Name ______________________

What Did the Story Say?

Use the words in the box to help you finish each sentence.

a kitten	carrots	a bunny	a puppy

Skipper is ______________.

Fluffy is ______________.

Nick will bring ______________ to the pet show.

Wiggles likes to nibble ______________.

Draw a picture of the pet you would bring to the pet show.
Write a sentence to tell what is special about your pet.

 Skills: Recall story details; relate personal experience to text.

Name ______________________________

Pick a Pronoun

Words that take the place of names are called **pronouns**.

Bunny likes to hop around the yard.
She hops through the grass.

Use the pronouns in the box to take the place of the words in **bold** letters.

We	He	She	They

My dog, **Max**, runs fast.

____________ likes to chase a ball.

I named my kittens **Huff and Puff**.

____________ look alike.

My parrot, **Polly**, can say my name.

____________ can sing, too.

Mom and I are at the pet store.

____________ want to buy a bunny.

Name ____________________

Correct the Capitals

Circle **yes** if the sentence begins with a capital letter.
Circle **no** if the sentence does not begin with a capital letter.
Fix the sentences that need capital letters.

My kitten is a good pet.	yes	no
it likes to play with string.	yes	no
the kitten got twisted up in the string.	yes	no
I had to help it.	yes	no
now my kitten is happy.	yes	no
what does your puppy like to play with?	yes	no
Do bunnies like to play?	yes	no
Every pet needs love.	yes	no

 Skill: Capitalize the first letter in a sentence.

Name ____________________

Find the Mystery Word

Do the crossword puzzle to find the mystery word.

Down

1. Nick's pet is a ____.
2. Fluffy likes to ____ and play.
3. Sara's pet is a ____.
6. Fluffy wears a ____.

Across

4. Skipper is a ____.
5. Wiggles likes to ____ carrots.
7. Skipper wags his ____.
8. My puppy ____ my face.

The mystery word is ____ ____ ____.

Skills: Recall information from text; develop vocabulary related to a theme; practice spelling.

Answer Key

Page 8
Drawings show a bunny, a blanket, and a book.

Drawing must show a boy.

Page 9
bun, sun, run, fun, spun

sun
bun
fun
run
spun

Page 10
Pictures are colored for: bib, book, bell, ball, bike, balloon, barn, bone

Page 11
bunk beds

Page 14
TV is circled.
Gramps, Mom are circled.

Drawings will vary.

Page 15
Pictures are marked for: trees, cheese, keys, skis, bees, peas

Page 16
on: lamp, car, dog, bird, stove
off: hat, coat, TV

Page 17
Drawings will vary.

Page 20

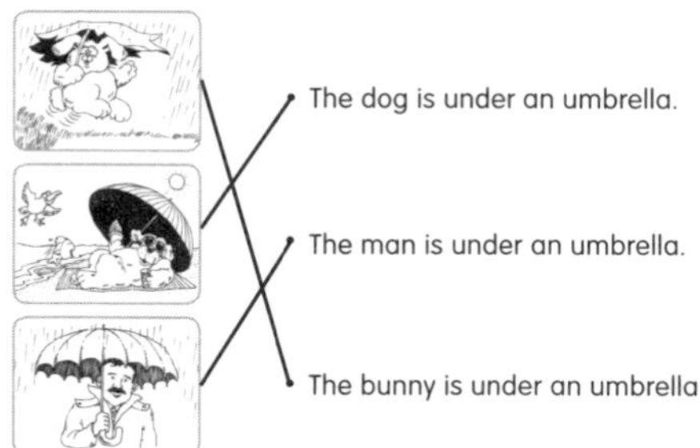

Drawings will vary.

Page 21

dog	frog
log	fog
jog	hog

Answers to questions will vary.

Page 22

under	on
on	under
under	on

Page 23
Umbrella is colored as labeled.
Drawings will vary.

Page 26
big fish
little fish
baby fish

Page 27
Pictures are colored for: swing, sweep, swim, swan, switch

Page 28
swim: shark, dog, turtle, jellyfish
fly: mosquito, butterfly, bat
swim and fly: duck

Page 29

fish	dish
wish	swish

Drawings will vary.

Page 32
Pictures are colored for: bugs, frog, ducks, fish, child

Drawings will vary.

Page 33

Page 34

yes	yes	no
no	yes	yes
yes	no	no

Page 35
Pictures are colored for: purse, pencil, parrot, penny, pizza, pig, puzzle

Page 38

Drawing shows monkeys eating bananas or other foods.

Page 39

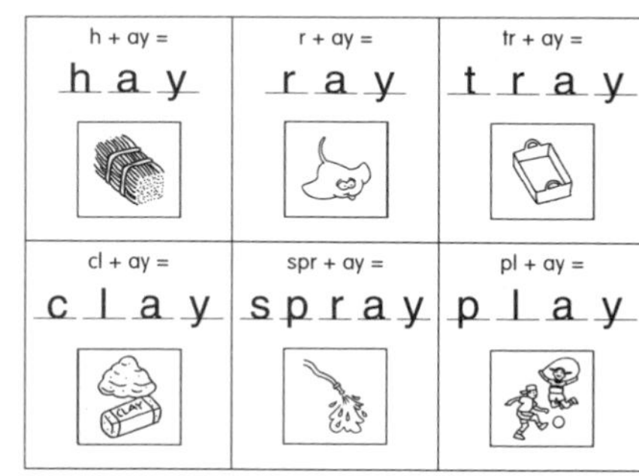

Words will vary.

Page 40

yes	no	yes
no	yes	no
no	no	yes
yes	no	no

Page 41
Drawings and foods will vary.

Page 44
home, butterfly, woodpile, hilltop

Page 45
take, cake, snake, rake, bake, lake

rake
take
bake, cake
snake, lake

Page 46
Pictures are colored for:
shell, shoes, shovel, sheep, shark, shamrock, shirt, ship

Page 47

cup + cake	wood + pile
butter + fly	bird + bath
hill + top	car + wash
bath + tub	

Page 50
hat: checkered
coat: striped
boots: spotted

Page 51
hat, rat
cat, bat
fat
flat

Drawings match the directions.

Page 52
Drawings will vary.

Page 53

Page 56
to a football game
to a movie
to the zoo
Answers will vary.

Drawings will vary.

Page 57
football, flag
"Coming Soon" poster, seats
"Lions" sign, lion cage

Popcorn is circled.

Page 58
popcorn
football
cupcake
bathtub
butterfly

1. cowboy
2. birthday
3. baseball

Page 59

Page 62
1. Do you have a bed?
2. Do you like milk and cookies?
3. Do you go to sleep?

Questions will vary.

Drawings must show a window and a star with a face.

Page 63
bed, Fred
Ted, red, sled
Ned, shed

Drawings match the directions.

Page 64
knight, kite
man, pan
star, car
bed, bread
snow, toe

Page 65
Answers will vary but must be in sentence form.

Questions and answers will vary.

Page 68
pajamas, toothbrush, blanket, teddy bear, socks, book, pillow

Page 69
sock, dock, lock, rock, clock, block

rock	lock
block	clock

Page 70
hard: book
soft: pillow, pajamas, teddy bear, socks, blanket
hard and soft: toothbrush

Page 71
Drawings will vary.

Page 74
1. Get a cup.
2. Mix pudding and milk.
3. Put on a lid.
4. Shake it up.
5. Take off the lid.
6. Eat it up.

Page 75
Answers may vary.

Page 76

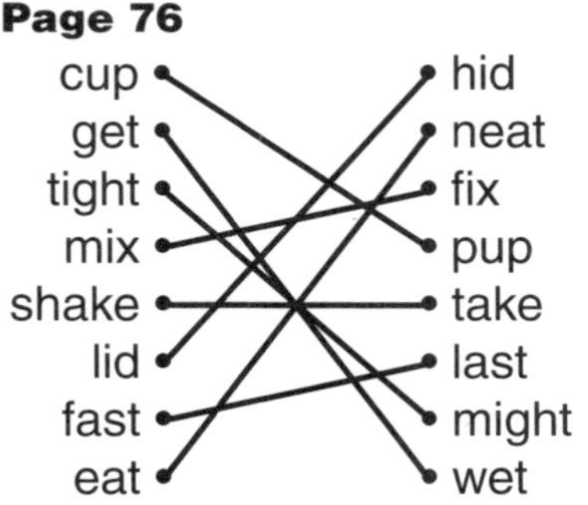

bet, get, wet
dog, log
Will, hill, Jill

Page 77
cupcake with a candle on it

Answers may vary.

Page 80
bag, box, dragon
rocks, shoe, duck
books, teacher, us

Page 81
bag, tag, rag, flag, drag, zag

bean**bag**
flagpole
dish**rag**
zig**zag**

Page 82

ba**g**	boo**t**
bu**s**	ma**n**
cu**p**	do**g**
ca**t**	ja**r**
ru**g**	tu**b**
bo**x**	boa**t**

Page 83
Wagon is made as directed.

Answers will vary.

Page 86
hay, horses
gas, food
ladders, hoses
blocks, toys

Page 87
heavy: truck, rock, books, wood
light: leaf, bag of feathers, basket, flowers

Page 88

1. farmer	4. teacher
2. builder	5. jumper
3. painter	6. player

5	1	2
3	6	4

Page 89

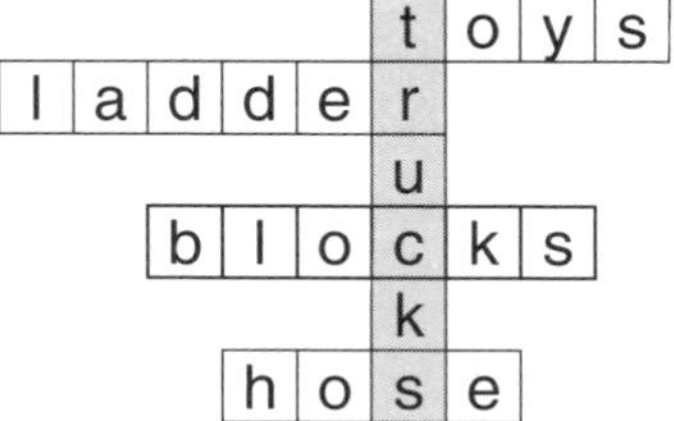

Mystery word: trucks

Page 92
Answers may vary but must contain story details.
Examples:
The boy is in the forest.
The boy is camping.
The campfire gives him heat and light.

Page 93
in the forest
a tent
over the campfire
ready
in his sleeping bag

Page 94
camp + fire
fire + fly
fire + place
fire + wood
fire + works
fire + fighter
fire + cracker
back + fire
fire + truck
fire + proof

Page 95
hear, keep, whispers, hoots, move, sleep

hear, fear
see, flee
toot, hoot

Page 98
pull the weeds
water the plants
good things to eat
yes
yes

Drawings and labels will vary.

Page 99

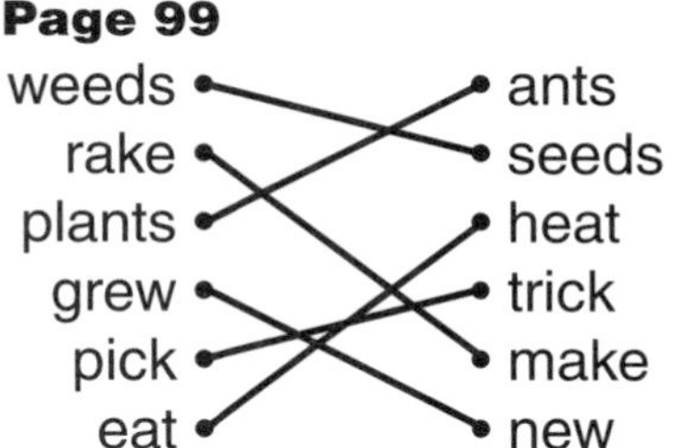

ants: plants
weeds: seeds
new: grew
rake: make

Page 100
Sentences will vary but must match the pictures.
Examples:
Rake the dirt.
Plant the seeds.
Water the plants.
Pick good things to eat.

Page 101

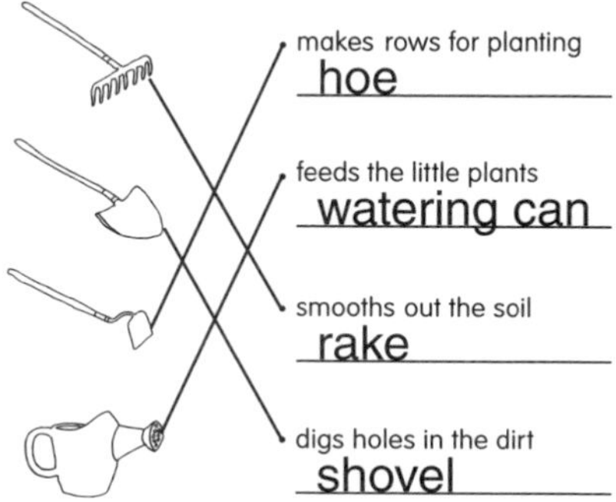

Page 104
It is a rainy day.

Rain is splattering on the sidewalk.

They can't play at the park, because it is raining.

They can jump in puddles and hide under an umbrella.

Answers will vary.

Page 105
hide, side, ride, tide, wide, slide, bride

hide, slide, ride, bride

Page 106
splash
splosh
splatter

Drawings will vary but must match the sentences.

Page 107
Lists will vary.
Drawings will vary.

Page 110
Answers will vary but must be in sentence form and include 3 of the following story details:

- lives at the North Pole
- walks on snow and ice
- has fur on the bottom of its feet
- is a good swimmer
- swims in icy water
- paddles with its front legs
- shakes the water off its fur

no—Answers will vary.

Page 111
bear, tear, wear, pear

wear, bear, pear, tear

Words and sentences will vary.

Page 112
run**n**ing, tap**p**ing, stop**p**ing, hit**t**ing, flip**p**ing

Sentences will vary but must include one of the **–ing** words above.

Double the final consonant in some words when you add **–ing**.

Page 113

Page 116
no
yes
yes
no
no
yes

Answers will vary.

Page 117
latch, batch, catch, hatch, match, patch, scratch

patch, catch, batch, match

Page 118
ran, flies, sailed, drives, blows

Words and tense may vary.
Examples:
eat, play, jumped, throws, flew

Page 119

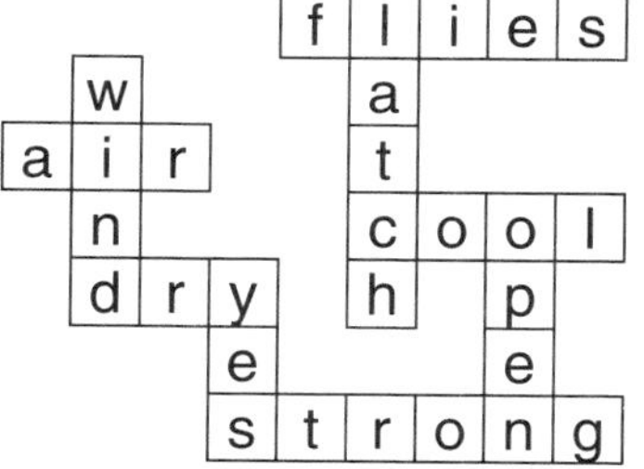

Page 122
Answers may vary but must include story details.
Examples:

A mouse, a bunny, a fox, and a ladybug moved into Sam's hat. The hat exploded.

All that was left was the little bell.

Hat is colored blue and drawing shows a mouse.

Page 123
first: mouse **second:** bunny
third: fox **fourth:** ladybug

Page 124
bunny's bunny
mouse's mouse
ladybug's ladybug
fox's fox
Sam's Sam

Page 125
biggest, bigger, big

bigger
biggest
big
bigger
biggest

Page 128
a puppy, a rug, kibble, a nap

Sparky**'s** dish
Sparky**'s** rug
Sparky**'s** kibble
Sparky**'s** nose

Page 129
at the pet store, in the yard, on the rug, on my lap

Page 130
on a dish of kibble.
and then give me a lick.
and takes a nap.

Words will vary but must rhyme with the word at the top of each column.

Page 131
Inside, outside, upside

yes
no
no
yes
no
yes
yes
no

Page 134
Answers will vary.

Page 135
I
I
me
I
me
I
me
I

Page 136
touch, smell, see, hear, jump, taste

smell
hear
ran

Page 137

fl**ag**	dr**ag**
sh**ow**	sn**ow**
dr**op**	sh**op**
ch**ick**	tr**ick**
br**ide**	sl**ide**
tr**ap**	cl**ap**
cl**own**	br**own**
sk**in**	ch**in**
sn**ake**	fl**ake**
sl**ate**	sk**ate**

Page 140

squirrel	inside its shell
frog	on a stick
turtle	in its hole
insect	on a leaf

Hiding helps keep the animals safe.

Answers may vary.
Answers may vary.
yes

Page 141
i, u, a, e

Page 142

Mystery word: hiding

Page 143
green frog on a green leaf
A frog hides on **a leaf**.

brown insect on a brown stick
A stick insect hides on **a stick**.

Page 146
Ingredients: bread, pickle, ham, lettuce

Drawings will vary.

What to do:
Wording may vary.
Example:
1. Start with a slice of bread.
2. Put a pickle on the bread.
3. Put ham over the pickle.
4. Put lettuce on the ham.
5. Put a slice of bread on top.

Page 147
slice, dice, mice, price, twice, spice

mice
price
dice
slice

Page 148
Answers will vary.

Page 149
Answers will vary.

Page 152
a puppy, a kitten, a bunny, carrots

Drawings and sentences will vary.

Page 153
He, They, She, We

Page 154
yes, no, no, yes, no, no, yes, yes

It likes to play with string.

The kitten got twisted up in the string.

Now my kitten is happy.

What does your puppy like to play with?

Page 155

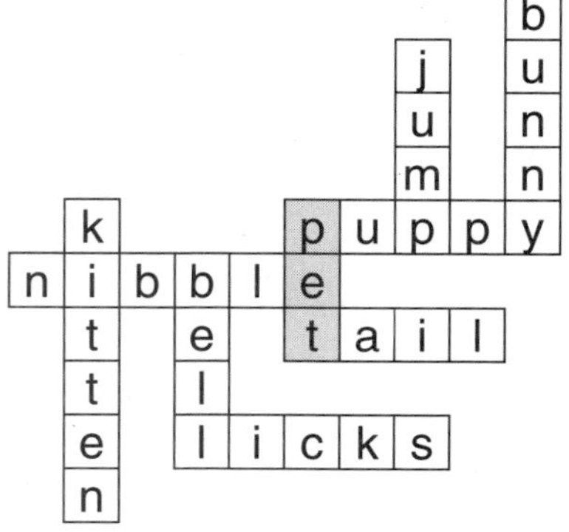

Mystery word: pet